YORK NOTES

General Editors: Professor A.N. Jeffares (*University of Stirling*) & Professor Suheil Bushrui (*American University of Beirut*)

George Eliot

SILAS MARNER

Notes by Anna Rutherford

BA (NEWCASTLE, N.S.W.)
*Head of Department of Commonwealth Literature
University of Aarhus*

 LONGMAN
YORK PRESS

YORK PRESS
Immeuble Esseily, Place Riad Solh, Beirut.

LONGMAN GROUP UK LIMITED
Longman House, Burnt Mill, Harlow,
Essex CM20 2JE, England
Associated companies, branches and representatives
throughout the world

© Librairie du Liban 1983

All rights reserved; no part of this publication may be reproduced,
stored in a retrieval system, or transmitted in any form or by any
means, electronic, mechanical, photocopying, recording, or otherwise
without either the prior written permission of the Publishers or a
licence permitting restricted copying in the United Kingdom issued by
the Copyright Licensing Agency Ltd, 90 Tottenham Court Road, London, W1P 9HE.

First published 1983
Eighth impression 1993

ISBN 0-582-02307-6

Produced by Longman Singapore Publishers Pte Ltd
Printed in Singapore

Contents

Part 1

Introduction

The life of George Eliot

George Eliot, whose real name was Mary Ann Evans, was born at Arbury Farm near Nuneaton in Warwickshire on 22 November 1819. She was the third child of Robert and Christiana Evans.

Robert Evans was a land agent and managed the estate of Francis Newdigate. When Mary Ann was four months old the family moved to another house on the estate. This was Griff House. It was situated in a very beautiful and quiet agricultural area much like the Raveloe of *Silas Marner*, yet not too far away was the beginning of an industrialised area similar to the one from which Silas Marner came. Her early life here was to play a vital role for it meant that many years later when she chose a rural setting for certain of her novels, namely *Silas Marner, The Mill on the Floss* and *Adam Bede*, George Eliot was able to draw on her childhood memories.

With her brother Isaac, of whom she was very fond, Mary Ann first of all attended Mrs Moore's dame school, but when she was only five she was sent to Miss Lathom's boarding school at Attleborough. Needless to say she was lonely and homesick and longed for holidays when she could be with her father and brother.

In 1828 Mary Ann changed schools. The principal of her new school was Maria Lewis, a believer in evangelical Christianity. She had a strong influence on Mary Ann, who became much more religiously fervent and conservative than the rest of her family who were conventional Anglicans.

In 1832, when she was thirteen, Mary Ann once more changed schools, for it was felt that she had learned all she could from Miss Lewis's school. This time she went to a school in Coventry run by Mary and Rebecca Franklin, daughters of Francis Franklin, the Minister of Cow Lane Baptist Chapel. Mary Ann's religious fervour was increased, she became more non-conformist and adopted the Calvinism of the Franklins. To show that she had renounced the world she took to wearing an extremely unbecoming cap on her head to make herself ugly. This was hardly necessary, for everyone, including Mary Ann herself, knew she was already ugly. Years later it was thought by many that she would marry Herbert Spencer (1820–1903), the famous social philosopher, but Spencer declared that even though he found Marian, as she was then called, 'the most admirable woman mentally he had ever met, he did not want to marry her because of her lack of beauty. He was in love with her, he said, but her long nose made her difficult to kiss. George Eliot's ugliness was a point of discussion for many. Another famous writer, Henry James (1843–1911) described her as 'magnificently ugly—deliciously hideous'. Her face was often compared to that of a horse and perhaps the unkindest description of all was when she was likened to 'an elderly Jewish cab-horse with ringlets'.

In 1836 Mary Ann's mother died and she was forced to leave school and look after her father and brother. At school Mary Ann had excelled at her lessons, particularly French, German, music and English composition. She continued with her studies at home, reading Italian, Greek and Latin, as well as German and French. In matters of religion she became even more devout and narrow-minded. She looked upon any entertainment as sinful and refused to accompany her brother to the theatre when they went to London. She herself later described this period as one when she used 'to go about like an owl'.

Another move was made in 1841 when she went with her father to live in Coventry. Mary Ann had continued to read widely and deeply, especially in the new philosophy and theology. This reading, and the influence of a new group of liberal friends in Coventry, especially Charles Bray, caused her to abandon her previous religious views. The entry in Robert Evans's diary for Sunday, 2 January reads, 'Went to Trinity Church in the forenoon ... Mary Ann did not go'. Her father refused to live with her if she would not go to church and for three weeks she stayed with her brother. Mary Ann then returned to her father's house and agreed to attend church with him, but she continued to reject all religious dogmas and remained an agnostic until her death.

Despite her rejection of traditional Christianity she retained her interest in theology and her first published work was a translation of David Friedrich Strauss's (1808–74) *Leben Jesu* (1835) (*The Life of Christ* in translated version, 1846). After the death of her father she went abroad for a certain period with the Brays, then she settled in London, where she became assistant editor of the *Westminster Review*, a liberal, intellectual periodical edited by John Chapman.

In London Marian, as she now called herself, was to meet the most brilliant writers and thinkers of the age, including Charles Dickens (1812–70), W. M. Thackeray, (1811–63), Lord Tennyson (1809–92), Thomas Carlyle (1795–1881), Charles Darwin (1809–82), and Herbert Spencer (1820–1903). Among them was George Henry Lewes (1817–78); he and Marian fell in love. Lewes was already married and although his wife had deserted him he was unable to get a divorce. Marian made up her mind that although she could not be legally married to George Lewes she would live with him as his wife. Her decision to do so was a very brave one for such things were not done in that age.

The typical reaction to what she and George Lewes did can be found in a letter from the sculptor Thomas Woolner (1826–92) to the painter William Bell Scott (1811–90). He asks Scott if he has heard what has happened and, in case he hasn't, tells him '[that] blackguard Lewes has bolted with a — and is living in Germany with her . . . I will not further lift the mantle and display the filthy contamination of these hideous satyrs and smirking moralists . . . stink pots of humanity'. 'Stink pots of humanity'. Mary Ann knew that this was the abuse that would be hurled at her but she decided to go ahead with something she did not believe was wrong. As Lord Acton (1834–1902) remarked, 'The sanctions of religion were indifferent to her after rejecting its doctrines and also, granted sufficient cause, she was prepared to disregard the social law of England.' It is ironical that Queen Victoria (1837–1901) gave her name to an age that is renowned for its narrowness, prudery and hypocrisy, yet she did not condemn George Eliot and her relationship with George Lewes. In a letter to her daughter Queen Victoria discussed liaisons where 'the outward earthly form cannot be given by man! In God's eyes,' the Queen wrote, 'I believe, as surely as I write this, that this will be considered as holy and right.' So did George Eliot! In a letter to Vincent Holbeche, her solicitor, she wrote, 'Our marriage is not a legal one, though it is regarded by us both as a sacred bond.'

In 1854 she and George Lewes went to Germany together and on their return lived happily as husband and wife until George Lewes's death in 1878. At first they were social outcasts, except amongst their free-thinking liberal friends, but eventually their relationship was accepted by all except a few. These included Marian's brother Isaac, who did not write to her for twenty-three years, the time she lived with George Lewes. A short while after George Lewes died Marian married John Cross but only eight months after they were married she died, on 22 December 1880.

George Eliot's literary career

Marian Evans had thought of herself as a critic and translator. It was George Lewes who persuaded her that her real gift lay in writing fiction and he encouraged her to do so. In 1857 her first story was published in *Blackwood's Magazine*. Two other stories appeared in the same magazine and in 1858 the three were published in book form under the title *Scenes from a Clerical Life*.

From the beginning Marian Evans wrote under the pseudonym of George Eliot, George because it was Lewes's name and Eliot because she liked the sound, 'a good mouth-filling word,' she said, 'easily pro-

Chapter I.

In the days when the spinning-wheels hummed busily
in the farm-houses, & even great ladies, clothed in silk
& thread lace, had their toy spinning-wheels of mahogany
or polished oak, there might be seen, in districts far-
away among the lanes or deep in the bosom of the
hills, certain pallid undersized men, who, by the
side of the brawny country folk, looked like the
remnants of a disinherited race. The shepherd's
dog barked fiercely when one of these alien-looking
men appeared on the upland, dark against the early
winter sunset; for what dog likes a figure bent under
a heavy bag? — & these pale men rarely stirred abroad
without that mysterious burthen. The shepherd himself,
though he had good reason to believe that the bag held
nothing but flaxen thread or else the long rolls of
strong linen spun from that thread, was not quite sure
that this trade of weaving, indispensable though it was,
could be carried on entirely without the help of the evil
one. In that far-off time superstition clung easily round
every person or thing that was at all unwonted,
or even intermittent & occasional merely, like the
visits of the pedlar or the knife-grinder. No one
knew where wandering men had their homes or

The first page of the manuscript of *Silas Marner*. MS.34026, f.4. Reproduced by permission of the British Library.

nounced'. Why did she decide to write under another name? Several suggestions have been put forward, all of which no doubt contain some degree of truth. First of all Marian Evans had thought of herself as a critic and she feared that people might disregard her criticism if they knew she wrote novels. The second reason, and most probably the major one, was the fear that people would refuse to buy the book of a woman living with a man to whom she was not married. She had good reason to believe this. People who had praised her work condemned it when they discovered that she was the author. Finally, and this was the reason for choosing a man's name, she wanted her books judged on their own merits and 'not', George Lewes said, 'prejudged as the work of a woman'.

Whilst people could not recognise the author they could recognise the talent of the writer. Her first book was the beginning of a success story that was to reach its highest peak on the publication of *Middlemarch* in 1871. This work was described then, and still is, as a 'masterpiece'. It was considered to be George Eliot's finest novel and she in turn was regarded as England's greatest living novelist, Dickens having died in 1870.

During her lifetime she enjoyed a very high reputation, but after her death there was a decline. The post-Victorian critics, in rejecting the narrow moral codes of the Victorian period, also rejected George Eliot's novels. What they failed to realise was that when she philosophised or made a moral judgement it was not based on any particular unchanging religious or social dogma. These she regarded as instruments of torture that 'rack and stretch' the soul. 'My function,' George Eliot said, 'is that of the *aesthetic*, not the doctrinal teacher—the rousing of nobler emotions, which mankind desire the social right, not the prescribing, of special measures.' The doctrine she believed in, and preached in her novels, was that of meliorism, a belief which affirms that the world may be made better by human effort. In his book *Religious Humanism and the Victorian Novel*, V. C. Knoepflmacher recounts that in 1853 Marian Evans told herself in a rare outburst of confidence: 'Heaven help us! said the old religions—the new one, from its very lack of that faith, will teach us all the more to help one another'. Nothing could be more radical than that; her religion was a socialist one of love, duty and self-sacrifice for the happiness of her fellow human beings on this earth.

It took the next generation of critics to realise this. The 1920s brought about a renewed interest in her novels. One of the persons responsible for this was another major English female novelist, Virginia Woolf (1882–1941). George Eliot's reputation has continued to increase. She was one of the few novelists that F. R. Leavis (1895–1978) included in his major work of criticism on the novel, *The Great Tradition* (1948), and today she is still quite rightly regarded as one of the greatest of the English novelists.

A note on the text

The edition of *Silas Marner* used for this critical guide is the Penguin English Library edition edited by Q. D. Leavis, Penguin Books, Harmondsworth, 1967. Students are recommended to use this edition if it is available. It contains an excellent introduction to *Silas Marner*, extensive notes, a note on dialect and a note on the text. The text of the Penguin edition is based on the one which appeared in 1868 in the complete edition of George Eliot's works. *Silas Marner* was first published in 1861.

The manuscript which George Eliot sent to the printer is in the British Museum (the first page of it is reproduced in these Notes). There are some alterations but not very many. One obvious alteration is the change in William's surname. Throughout the manuscript he is called William Waif but in the first printed edition 'Waif' has been changed to 'Dane'. George Eliot must have changed it in the proof copy she received from the printer. The other notable change is the omission of 'story' from the title page which originally read 'Silas Marner, the Weaver of Raveloe, A Story by George Eliot'. George Eliot insisted that 'story' be removed in case people thought it a mere entertainment and not the serious work of art she intended it to be. Generally there are very few changes in the manuscript and when they occur they are for the better. There were a number of editions of *Silas Marner* during George Eliot's lifetime but she made no attempt to alter the original. In a letter written in 1872 she comments: 'When a subject has begun to grow in me, I suffer terribly until it has wrought itself out—become a complete organism; and then it seems to take wing and go away from me. *That* thing is not to be done again—that life has been lived'.

Part 2

Summaries
of SILAS MARNER

A general summary

Silas Marner is a weaver who lives in a cottage on the outskirts of the village of Raveloe. He is regarded with suspicion by the people of Raveloe for a number of reasons: his trade, the fact that he comes from the town, looks different from the rest of the community, sometimes suffers from fits, has a knowledge of certain herbs that can cure some diseases, and refuses to mix with the rest of the community.

Fifteen years before Silas had been living in the town where he was a member of a small religious sect, called the Lantern Yard Community. Silas was an extremely honest, simple man who had complete faith in God and the people in his community. He is betrayed by his so-called 'best friend', William Dane, and is accused of stealing money. The money was actually stolen by William himself, at a moment when Silas was unconscious, because he was suffering from one of the fits to which he was occasionally subject. Silas declares his innocence and agrees to the matter being settled by a drawing of lots, a method of testing guilt or innocence, which the religious community believe is sanctioned by the Bible. The lots declare Silas to be guilty, and Silas, knowing himself to be innocent, leaves the town, having lost all faith in God and man.

For fifteen years Silas has lived a lonely life in Raveloe where he has gained the reputation of being a miser. His only aim now is to amass money, not because of what it can buy him, but simply to provide him with a purpose in life. He works day and night and becomes fanatical about earning more gold coins. He keeps his gold in a bag in a hole in the floor of his cottage and takes it out every night to count.

The richest and most important man in the village is Squire Cass. He has two sons, Dunstan and Godfrey. Dunstan is a thoroughly bad fellow; Godfrey is not bad, but he is weak. He has made an unfortunate and secret marriage with a woman called Molly Farren who is a drug addict. Dunstan knows about this and is blackmailing Godfrey. If Godfrey will not give him money he threatens that he will go to their father and tell him about Godfrey's marriage. Godfrey is frightened that the Squire will disinherit him, so he agrees to let Dunstan sell his, Godfrey's, horse Wildfire, in order to get money. Dunstan, acting foolishly, kills the horse. He returns through the fog to Raveloe and comes across Silas Marner's cottage. The door is open and the room empty, so Dunstan enters and steals the gold.

When Silas returns he finds his money gone. He is completely heart-broken, and, not knowing what to do, he goes to the Rainbow Inn and seeks the help of the villagers. They are kind and sympathetic towards him and suggest that it was a pedlar who stole the money.

On New Year's Eve Squire Cass holds a party at his home, the Red House. All the important people attend including Nancy Lammeter. Godfrey loves Nancy and wants to marry her but cannot, because he is already married. Nancy does not know this. Whilst the party is taking place Molly Farren is struggling through the snow with her baby. She intends to go to the Red House and reveal the truth. On the way, however, she is overcome by drugs and falls down and dies in the snow. Her little girl finds her way to Silas's cottage. The door is open, she toddles in and falls asleep in front of the fire. Silas does not notice, because he is having one of his fits. When he wakes, he thinks at first that his gold has returned, then he realises it is the golden hair of a little girl. He finds her mother and goes to the Red House to announce his discovery. Godfrey realises it is his wife and child; he is terrified that his wife is not dead, and is relieved when he learns that she is. Silas announces that he will keep the child. Again Godfrey is relieved, because to own her as his daughter would mean acknowledging his past marriage. And this might mean the loss of both his inheritance and Nancy Lammeter, whom he is now free to marry.

Silas christens the little girl Eppie and brings her up as his own daughter. Once more he has a purpose in life and is gradually re-integrated into a community, this time the village of Raveloe. The whole village loves Eppie and respects Silas for taking her in. He is no longer feared.

Sixteen years later the stone pit, which is next to Silas's cottage, is drained and the skeleton of Dunstan and Silas's money are found. The thief is revealed. Godfrey tells Nancy about his brother and also about his first unhappy marriage. Nancy and Godfrey have no children and they agree to adopt Eppie. Eppie, however, refuses to leave the only father she has ever known. Godfrey is forced to accept this as a punishment for his neglect of his duty many years before.

The story ends with the marriage of Eppie to Aaron Winthrop. They will live with Silas, who, through his love of the child, has been restored to his faith in man and God.

Detailed summaries

Chapter 1

We are introduced to Silas Marner, the hero and main character in the novel. Silas is a weaver and when we meet him he is living on the outskirts of the village of Raveloe near a deserted stone-pit.

The villagers are simple people who regard Silas with suspicion. There are a number of reasons for this. Even though Raveloe lies quite close to the industrialised area where Silas comes from, it has not yet been touched by mechanisation and industrialisation. Silas therefore is an alien in two ways; he comes from the town, and he is a man with a trade, a weaver. Not only has he skill as a weaver but he also knows about certain herbs which have the power to cure. His appearance also sets him apart; compared to the villagers he is 'pallid' and 'undersized', he has 'large brown protuberant eyes' and always appears to be peering (he is short-sighted). The boys of the village are afraid of him and this fear is increased when one day Jem Rodney meets Silas whilst he is having a fit. We know it to be a fit, but to the villagers it is a further sign of strangeness. This confirms their belief that perhaps Silas has supernatural powers and causes them to fear him slightly. It is this fear that saves Silas from persecution. They are content to let him live his life in peace, mixing with no one and never speaking to anyone unless he has to. When we first meet Silas he has lived in Raveloe for fifteen years and during that time has amassed a great amount of money.

The second part of Chapter 1 tells us why Silas first came to Raveloe and helps to explain the reason for his present attitude to people and to life. Before Silas came to Raveloe he had been a member of a narrow religious sect in the town. He was a devout and honest man and was engaged to an equally good woman, Sarah. Silas had a special position within the church because at one of the meetings he had fallen into a trance, similar to the one in which Jem Rodney saw him, and the sect thought this to be a special sign of grace from God. Only one man in the sect suggested that this might indicate the influence of Satan and not God, and that was William Dane who was supposed to be Silas Marner's closest friend.

The senior deacon of the church fell dangerously ill and, as he had no family to care for him, the various members of the church, including William and Silas, took turns to look after him. One night whilst watching over him, Silas obviously fell into one of his trances and when he woke the deacon was dead. Later in the day Silas was summoned to the church and accused of robbing the deacon. His knife had been found in the drawer at the deacon's, and the empty purse which had contained the deacon's money was found in Silas's house. Silas denied the charge and remembered that the last time he had used the knife was to cut a strap for William. He realises that William is the guilty one, but does not accuse him because his trust in God is so great that he believes that God will prove him innocent. Because of this trust he agrees to a drawing of lots to prove whether he is innocent or guilty. The lots say he is guilty. Silas then accuses William and declares that 'there is no just God that governs the earth righteously, but a God of lies, that bears witness against the innocent'. The next day Sarah breaks off the engagement (she marries William Dane little more than a month later), and shortly afterwards Silas leaves the town and goes to live in isolation and bitterness at Raveloe.

COMMENTARY: In this chapter George Eliot sets the scene. The events of *Silas Marner* take place during the Napoleonic Wars (1793–1815), which means that Silas arrived in Raveloe at the end of the 1780s. Although there is only one specific reference to time ('In the early years of this century') there are other less obvious clues that help tell us when the events are taking place, for instance, 'in the days when the spinning wheels hummed busily in the famhouses'. Each housewife would spin her own yarn and then have such people as Silas weave it for her. It was a time when the individual craftsman had not yet been replaced by the factory and the machine.

When the book ends, sixteen years have elapsed, and there are clues that this is what is happening. At the time when we meet Silas there were small pockets of industrialisation but these were not common. Most of England still lived in much the same manner as the villagers at Raveloe and this explains why Silas is looked upon as an alien. The simple village person was a superstitious person who was much more willing to believe that cleverness was a sign of the Devil rather than a sign of God. Even today many people feel that there is a touch of the Devil in cleverness; a good man is not a clever man. In a flashback we are taken back fifteen years to when Silas lived as a happy member of the small Lantern Yard community. The betrayal by his best friend and the seeming betrayal by God and the community provide the reason for his presence in Raveloe and the psychological reason for his shunning of mankind.

NOTES AND GLOSSARY:

tread-mill: a large wheel with steps inside it. The man was placed inside it; when he put his foot on the step, the step and the wheel went down. If the man wanted to remain upright, he had to keep on treading and this forced the wheel round. The tread-mill was once used as an instrument of punishment

chary of his time: he did not want to waste his time

turnpike: a turnpike was a barrier placed across a road so that the coach could be stopped and a toll collected. Turnpikes were only on the major roads

David and Jonathan: a reference to two characters from the Bible, the Old Testament (1. *Samuel* 18:4), who were very good friends

'calling and election sure': these words are from the Bible, the New Testament (2. *Peter* 1:10–11). It was the belief of certain people that God had called them and that they were sure of election to eternal life, that is, they were certain to be saved and go to Heaven

Chapter 2

In Chapter 1 we saw how the villagers looked upon Silas as an alien. In this chapter the position is reversed and we see that Silas looks at the village and its inhabitants in the same way. For even though the town and the Lantern Yard community are in reality only a very short way from Raveloe, it could, because of many differences, be another world.

With the loss of his friends and his belief in God, Silas feels that life, past, present and future, holds nothing for him. All he has left is his weaving, and he devotes himself so completely to it that he becomes little more than 'a spinning insect'.

One opportunity arises that might make the villagers accept him. He recognises that one of the villagers, Sally Oates, is suffering from the same disease as his mother. His instinct to do good asserts itself, he feels pity and he takes Sally Oates a herbal remedy his mother had used for the same complaint. The result is that Sally Oates finds relief and the village finds Silas stranger still! He seems to possess magical charms.

Silas is now besieged by the village women wanting to be cured of all kinds of diseases. If Silas had not been the kind of man he was he could have made a lot of money, but being honest, he tells them truthfully that he is not a wise man able to cure disease. The villagers disbelieve him, they think he deliberately refuses to cure them, and he is looked upon with even greater fear and suspicion.

With this incident goes the last chance for Silas to have companions. From now on he becomes a miser whose sole purpose in life is to amass wealth. His one joy is to count his coins, which he does every evening before he goes to bed. At first he keeps them in an iron pot, but this eventually is not big enough so he makes two leather bags for his coins. These he keeps in a hole in the floor which he covers with bricks and sawdust each time he replaces the coins.

Living such a life Silas becomes withered and old. He looks much older than his forty years, and the children call him 'Old Master Marner'.

This is the pattern of Silas's life for fifteen years till just before Christmas in the year we first meet him. An event then occurs that is to change the pattern of his life once more.

COMMENTARY: This chapter begins with a general statement about the psychological effect of people who are suddenly transported to a new land or region and lose all contact with their old way of life. It is obvious that it is the author speaking and that she is presenting a certain point of view which she wishes her readers to share with her. This is a technique known an authorial intrusion; it was also used by other Victorian novelists.

After making a general proposition George Eliot goes on to illustrate it with a particular example, in this case through Silas Marner. The gap between the world of the artisan in the town and the farmer in the village is emphasised and used to account for the feeling of alienation that Silas endures. His final and complete alienation is brought about by the villagers' reaction to his act of kindness. This confirms Silas's distrust of man and reveals George Eliot's insight into human psychology.

Having no outlet for human love Silas turns to a cold inanimate object, gold. That this is a negative thing to love is reflected in the physical condition of Silas. The fact that he withers physically is symbolic; such a love is life-destroying. There is one small positive note: his grief when his favourite pot breaks. This incidates that his feelings have not been completely destroyed.

NOTES AND GLOSSARY:
Lethean influence: an influence that causes forgetfulness. In classical mythology Lethe was a river of the underworld; those who drank its waters forgot their former life on earth

occult: secret, beyond the bounds of natural knowledge

amulet: a charm which protects the wearer

couplets of the hymn as it was given out: in those days many people could not read. Therefore the preacher read the words of the hymn a couplet (two lines) at a time and the people repeated it after him

wholesale dealer: in this instance the wholesale dealer is the middle man. Silas and weavers like him did the work, but they did not sell it directly to the persons who were buying it. Instead they gave it to the wholesale dealer who paid the weavers a wage and then sold the cloth to customers. The wages paid to the weavers were a good deal less than the wholesale dealer got for the cloth. The difference he kept for himself. At Raveloe there is no wholesale dealer or middle man; Silas sells directly to his customers and gets more money

the Wise Woman: a witch
the water in the head: a disease more commonly known as 'water on the
brain'

Chapter 3

The richest and greatest man in the village is Squire Cass who lives in the
Red House with his four sons. Because his wife died many years before,
Squire Cass spends a lot of his time at the inn, too much time in the opinion
of many of the villagers. They think it wrong of the Squire to allow his sons
to remain idle and they are particularly worried about his eldest son,
Godfrey, who recently seems to be following the same path as his brother
Dunstan, who is also called Dunsey. The villagers do not care about
Dunstan who gambles, drinks and is thoroughly wicked. But they feel that
Godfrey is basically a good man and that there is hope for him if he were to
marry Nancy Lammeter, the highly respected and beautiful daughter of
Mr Lammeter.

We meet the two brothers in their father's home and they are
quarrelling. Godfrey is demanding a hundred pounds from his brother.
This is money that he received from Fowler, one of his father's tenants,
and which he lent to Dunsey, instead of giving it to his father. The Squire
thinks that Fowler has not paid, and is threatening to sue him. Therefore
Godfrey must find one hundred pounds. Dunsey, however, refuses to
repay the money, and we learn the reason for his power over Godfrey, why
Godfrey is unhappy, and why he does not marry Nancy Lammeter even
though he loves her. In a moment of passion Godfrey married a drunken
woman, Molly Farren. Dunstan knows about this marriage, indeed we
are led to believe that, out of spite and hatred, he trapped Godfrey into it;
and now he threatens to tell the Squire if Godfrey does not give him
money. For one moment Godfrey can no longer bear the deceit and
Dunstan's blackmail and decides that he will tell his father everything.
On second thoughts, however, he realises he cannot bear to lose his
inheritance—his father would turn him out—and Nancy Lammeter. So
he agrees to the proposal that Dunstan will take Wildfire, Godfrey's horse,
to Batherley, the neighbouring market town, the next morning and sell
it. There are two reasons why Godfrey does not go himself: Molly
Farren lives in Batherley, and, if he remains in Raveloe the next day, he
can meet Nancy Lammeter.

COMMENTARY: Chapter 3 introduces the second plot, which revolves
around Godfrey Cass, and which interacts with the other plot that is
centred on Silas Marner.

Once again George Eliot draws a distinction between the established
Church (Anglican) and the non-conformists (Puritans).

We are told about the social structure of Raveloe and many other parts of England which were still untouched by 'industrial energy' and 'Puritan earnestness'. The rich took for granted their right to be rich and the poor accepted it. If the rich ate well then it was all the better for the poor for there would be more 'orts' (food left over and given to them).

NOTES AND GLOSSARY:

Napoleonic Wars: the people of Raveloe called it the glorious war-time because, as is always the case in war, those who supply the armies, whether it be with weapons or food, are able to make a great profit

orts: food left over from a meal which is given to the poor

pillion: seat for a second rider behind the rider of the horse. The groom rode the horse and the lady rode pillion

cheries: an animal's backbone or a part of it used as a joint of meat

spun butter: butter which has been worked into a thread-like consistency so that it can be used for ornamental purposes, just as icing is used today to decorate cakes

wild oats: to sow one's wild oats means to lead a life of pleasure and gaiety before settling down

King George: King George III (1760–1820). *Silas Marner* takes place during the reign of George III

turn over a new leaf: change his habits

foxes' brushes: the tail of the fox was kept as a trophy

cut off with a shilling: to be disinherited

haven't a shilling to bless myself with: this expression dates from the time when a cross was stamped on the coins

laudanum: a liquid made from opium

sword hanging over him: this refers to the sword of Damocles. Damocles envied Dionysius, ruler of Syracuse (430–367 BC). Dionysius knew this and at a feast he ordered Damocles to sit in his (Dionysius's) chair. Over the chair was a sword suspended by a single hair, to show Damocles how dangerous a life a ruler led

crooked sixpence: a crooked sixpence was supposed to bring good luck

riot: here, riotous living

vicinage: vicinity, in the neighbourhood

Chapter 4

The next morning Dunstan Cass sets off for the hunt where he plans to sell Wildfire. On the way he passes Silas Marner's cottage. He thinks about all the money Silas must have and how this money could solve Godfrey's problem. He decides that when he returns he will frighten Silas into lending him the money.

Dunstan goes to the hunt and sells the horse for one hundred and twenty pounds. The sensible thing would be to deliver the horse and collect the money, but he is vain as well as greedy and stupid, and therefore decides to ride in the hunt. Through Dunstan's foolishness the horse falls and dies. Dunstan is now without money or horse, and has to walk home through ever-thickening fog. When he is only three-quarters of a mile from his own home he sees a light. This comes from Silas Marner's cottage. The way is difficult because of the mist, dark and rain, but he manages to reach the door of the cottage. He knocks and enters to find the cottage empty. The fire is lit, there is food cooking, but Silas is nowhere to be seen. Dunstan thinks it is possible that Silas has fallen down the stone pit; then the miser's money must belong to anyone who finds it, which means, of course, himself. He quickly searches the cottage, finds the two bags of gold and stumbles out with them, into the dark night.

COMMENTARY: We are presented in this chapter with a set of circumstances and events which are to join the plot of Silas Marner to that of Godfrey Cass. Everything is carefully and logically planned and hinges very much on the character of Dunstan. His greed and wickedness are the cause of his journey to the hunt and of his fatal end. His vanity leads him to stake Wildfire and to return to Raveloe along lonely back roads. He stumbles across the cottage of Silas and his greed asserts itself once more. The absence of Silas from the cottage and the reason why the door is open is again logically explained. The grimness of Dunstan's act is matched by the weather which also plays a vital role in the outcome of the events in this chapter.

Note the nice touch of irony when Dunstan thinks that one reason why Silas is absent is perhaps because he has fallen into the stone pit.

NOTES AND GLOSSARY:

obliged to ride to cover on his hunter: because Dunstan has only one horse he is obliged to ride it to the hunt. Normal practice was for the huntsman to ride another horse to the meet (hunt) whilst his groom led his hunter so that it would be fresh for the event

to cover: the hunt or the meet, cover from covert, which is the area of thick undergrowth in which the fox hides

got more blood: is a better breed

pocket pistol: a hip flask. It was common to carry a flask or bottle of spirits in one's hip pocket

coppice:	a small area of trees and underwood which is cut down periodically
too pale a colour:	they were silver, not gold
cajoling:	flattering
jacks:	a jack is an instrument used to turn a spit. It is so called because it saved the labour of a jack, or boy

Chapter 5

Silas has left his cottage to get some twine which he needs to set up a new piece of work. He would have fetched it the next morning but that would have meant time lost in weaving which in turn would mean less money. So in spite of the very bad weather he goes out that evening. He has not locked the door of his house because the string that was around his piece of meat was also attached to the key. And besides, there has been no thief in fifteen years, so why should one decide to come now, and on such a night?

On his return all seems as he had left it and he prepares to enjoy the piece of meat he has been given. It was his practice to count his gold after he had eaten, but this evening he decides to set it on the table so that he can look at it whilst having his meal and have the double pleasure of enjoying his food and his gold. Going to the hiding place he realises with horror that his gold has vanished. At first he cannot believe that this is true; perhaps he has hidden it in some other place. Finally, however, he is forced to admit that his gold has gone, and when he faces this truth the desolation he feels is as great as when his former friends and God had deserted him. Once again his purpose in life has been destroyed, and he asks himself whether an evil spirit is persecuting him or a thief. Silas thinks that it would be easier to catch a thief than an unknown spirit, so he decides it is a thief, and his suspicion falls on Jem Rodney, the mole-catcher and poacher. He decides to go to the Rainbow Inn, tell of the robbery, and trust that the Squire and other great men of the village will help him to recover his money.

COMMENTARY: George Eliot is anxious to point out that in spite of his greed for gold and his growing worship of it Silas remains at heart a simple man, a good man free of vice who could never perform any act that would injure another human being. There is a sharp contrast here with Dunstan Cass; one man is innately good, the other innately wicked. Both desire gold, but the cause of their desire is different, and the ends they will go to to obtain it are sharply contrasted. One works for it, the other steals. In spite of all he has suffered, Silas's confidence in man is not completely shattered. We realise this when he turns to the village people to seek their help.

NOTES AND GLOSSARY:

horn lantern: the lantern Silas had was made out of horn. This was a common practice before glass became cheap enough for general use

Chapter 6

The scene is the Rainbow tavern where the less prosperous villagers are sitting in the kitchen, drinking, smoking and discussing the life and interests of the village. Bob, the butcher, has a disagreement with Mr Dowlas, the farrier, over a red Durham cow. When their argument becomes a little heated, Mr Snell, the landlord and peacemaker, changes the conversation.

Their next topic for discussion is the deputy-clerk's inability to sing. Once again Mr Snell is the peacemaker; he comes to poor Mr Tooley's rescue and changes the conversation once more by getting old Mr Macey, the tailor and village clerk, to recount stories from the past about the Lammeters, the house where they live, and why it is called Charity Lands. The reason for this name is that the previous owner had left the property to a London charity. He was a London tailor called Cliff and was a strange man who went raving mad before he died. Some believed that on certain occasions, which they called Cliff's holidays, the Devil let him out of Hell to visit the grand, and now deserted, stables that he had built. This conversation leads to a discussion about the existence or non-existence of ghosts and it is at this point that Silas Marner enters the inn.

COMMENTARY: This chapter is considered by many critics as one of the finest in English literature. George Eliot has been rightly praised for her ear for dialogue and her splendid presentation of the villagers of Raveloe. It is the one and only time in the novel that we are to meet them as individuals in their own right and is a superb example of character portrayal in which George Eliot reveals her deep insight into character. As we listen to their conversation, in the rich dialect of the area, we learn not only about the character of each individual but also about the beliefs and superstitions of the village.

There is a warmth and humour in this communal scene which stands out in sharp contrast to the previous scene where the lone Silas stands bereft of all he possesses.

NOTES AND GLOSSARY:

fustian jackets: fustian is a thick strong coarse cotton cloth made of a mixture of flax and cotton dyed a dull neutral colour. It was the material the labourers used most often for their clothing

smock frock: a loose-fitting outer garment of coarse white linen worn by labourers over their other clothes

drenching: forcing medicine down an animal's throat

Queen's heads: after Queen Anne died in 1714 the coins were embossed with the head of George I but Queen Anne coins remained in circulation for some time after her death

Old Harry: the Devil

reasonable: in the dialect used here 'to have reason' means 'to be right'. Notice that Mr Macey said that January was an 'unreasonable' month to marry in, that is, not the right month; for Raveloe the 'reasonable' time for marriage is Spring

Chapter 7

The villagers are startled by the appearance of Silas, whom, for one moment, they take to be a ghost. Silas cries out that he has been robbed and accuses Jem Rodney. Jem denies the charge, and the others warn Silas that he must not make false accusations. Silas remembers how he himself was wrongly accused and apologises to Jem Rodney. Some think that because of the mysterious nature of the theft—there is no evidence of a thief being there—it was the Devil himself who has stolen the money, and that this means that the Devil has broken his friendship with Marner. Mr Dowlas, the farrier, however, is more practical, and declares that if one looked carefully they would find clues and that it is only because Silas is short-sighted that he has not seen them. He suggests that he go with Silas to Mr Kench, the constable, who is sick, and get himself sworn in as deputy constable. Then he and Silas can go to the cottage and make further investigations. Mr Macey objects that the farrier cannot be a constable because he is a doctor, even if he is only a cow doctor. Once more there is argument and once more the landlord steps in and creates peace. It is agreed that Mr Dowlas should go, but not as an official. So Silas, Mr Dowlas and the landlord go out into the dark, wet night once more.

COMMENTARY: This is a significant moment for Silas. Previously his love and worship of gold had led him to fear and reject the company of other men, 'His gold, as he hung over it and saw it grow, gathered his power of loving together into a hard isolation like its own'. Now, in complete desperation, he turns to the people he has shunned and avoided for fifteen years. It is the beginning of a process of reconciliation with his fellow men, a process of which he is scarcely aware at first, for, as George Eliot says, 'Our consciousness rarely registers the beginning of a growth within us any more than without us: there have been many circulations of the sap before we detect the smallest sign of the bud' (Chapter 7). The change in Silas is matched by a change in the villagers. Seeing him in his distress they forget their distrust and suspicion of him and regard him with the same pity and compassion as they would any other villager. The robbery has acted as a catalyst in the transformation of Silas.

NOTES AND GLOSSARY:

mushed: a dialect word meaning depressed, crushed. A musher is an instrument used for crushing

nolo episcopari: a Latin phrase meaning 'I do not want to be a bishop'. In former times when the king offered the bishopric to a priest, the priest was supposed to say twice 'I do not want to be a bishop'. This was simply a formality and when the king asked him the third time he accepted. It is now used as a phrase to indicate pretended unwillingness

Chapter 8

Next morning everyone in the village is talking about the robbery. Some of the villagers are so suspicious of Silas that they think he could have stolen the money himself, though they can give no reasons for his doing so. A tinder-box is found, and suspicion then falls on a pedlar who has been in the village about a month before.

Godfrey goes to the Rainbow and hears about the robbery, but is far more interested in what has happened to Dunsey and his horse Wildfire. He decides to ride to Batherley but on the way meets Bryce, one of the men who had wanted the horse. Bryce tells Godfrey what happened to his horse and reports that Dunsey, who was not hurt, has disappeared.

Godfrey decides that there is nothing else to do but to make a full confession to his father the next morning and hope that, in his desire to save the family's pride and reputation, his father will hush the matter up. He goes to bed with that resolution but when he wakes up he cannot go through with it. Once more he puts his trust in chance and hopes that something will turn up to save him.

COMMENTARY: Again George Eliot reveals how superstitious the villagers are and how willing they are to suspect outsiders. They immediately jump to the conclusion that it must be the pedlar who has stolen Silas's money though there is no evidence that he has.

Godfrey once more shows himself to be a weak and indecisive man. George Eliot criticises both the Squire and Godfrey in this chapter, the Squire because he spoils Godfrey ('faulty indulgence') and Godfrey because he accepts this as 'natural enough'.

NOTES AND GLOSSARY:

tinder-box: before matches were invented light was made by striking a piece of steel with a flint. This created a spark which set fire to the tinder, dry material which easily caught light. The tinder, flint and steel were all carried in the tinder-box

they're o' King George's making: the constables and justices of the peace were appointed in the reign of King George III

clairvoyante: a woman who is supposed to be able to see things not present to the senses

---

Chapter 9

The next morning Godfrey tells his father that Fowler has paid his rent but that Godfrey has lent it to Dunstan instead of giving it to him. Because Dunstan refused to repay the money Godfrey arranged for him to sell Wildfire so he could pay back the money. Unfortunately Wildfire has been killed and Dunstan has failed to return. The Squire is very angry and suspects that Dunstan has some hold over Godfrey, for why else would Godfrey lend him the Squire's money. Godfrey is terrified that his father has come so close to the truth, but he denies it, and says that Dunstan knows about some foolish prank which is of no concern to his father. The Squire then speaks to Godfrey about marrying Nancy Lammeter, and tells him that, if Godfrey will not ask Nancy, then he, the Squire, will ask Nancy's father. Godfrey begs him not to do that, and assures his father that he will ask Nancy, but not just now. Godfrey leaves his father hardly knowing whether he is better or worse off than before. His only hope is that good fortune will smile on him. Once more he puts his faith in Chance.

COMMENTARY: 'Favourable Chance is the god of all men who follow their own devices instead of obeying a law they believe in'. In this chapter George Eliot reveals her attitude to the lazy, dishonest, unreliable and weak men who ignore the law, the social and moral codes, and substitute Chance for their god. But, she reminds us, a certain seed brings forth a certain fruit and the god of Chance has no power to change this. This is a lesson that Godfrey has yet to learn.

NOTES AND GLOSSARY:

unstring: to undo the string around their purses

the newspaper's talking about peace: this is a further reference to the Napoleonic Wars. See note on this in Chapter 3

Prices 'ud run down like a jack: if the war were to end, prices would sink like a clockwork machine when the spring is released. See the note on jack, Chapter 4

collogue: to conspire, to plot

my property's got no entail on it: if there was entail on a property it meant that there was a predetermined order of succession and the people in this line of succession could not be disinherited. Since the time of Squire Cass's grandfather there has been no entail on the Red House, which means the Squire can disinherit Godfrey and leave it to whom he likes

shilly-shally: to be undecided (from 'shall I, shall I' which originally was 'shill I, shall I')

Chapter 10

Justice Mallam believes that the tinder-box is a clue to the robbery and orders an inquiry to try to find the suspect pedlar. This inquiry is unsuccessful. No one thinks of connecting the disappearance of Dunstan Cass with the robbery. When the villagers speak about the robbery, they are still divided. Some believe that the pedlar has stolen it, others still think that supernatural forces are responsible.

Silas is completely filled with grief and pain. To the outsider it appeared that Silas's life had been one without joy and without any reason to live. But this was not the case. His money had provided a purpose in life for him. Now that this is gone he is completely broken and has not the will to begin again.

But his loss has changed the villagers' attitude towards him. They realise now that if he has avoided them until now, it was not because he disliked them, or had something against them, but because he was perhaps a little crazy. If he had not helped them before it was not because he would not, but because he could not.

To show him that they are sympathetic and feel more kindly towards him they bring him small gifts of food. Those who have no food to offer call to see him to try to cheer him up. Two of his visitors are Mr Macey and Mrs Winthrop. Having assured Silas that he does not think he is in league with the Devil, Mr Macey advises him to have a Sunday suit made and go to church. This is the same advice given him by Dolly Winthrop, the wheelwright's wife, a good woman who loves doing good and helping those who suffer. She visits Silas with her seven-year-old son, Aaron, and asks Silas about his church-going habits. Silas replies that he has never been to church, only to chapel. Chapel is a word unknown to Mrs Winthrop, but she does not ask its meaning in case it might be a place of wickedness. Instead she urges Silas to go to church, particularly as it is the Christmas season.

In spite of the persuasions of Mr Macey and Mrs Winthrop, Silas does not go to church on Christmas day, nor does he join in the village celebrations. Instead he stays at home and spends a cold, lonely Christmas by himself.

In the Red House Christmas is celebrated, but the grander party is to take place on New Year's Eve when everyone of importance will come for the celebrations. Godfrey is looking forward to it very much as he can be with Nancy Lammeter. He has, however, two worries. His wife is blackmailing him for money and he fears that Dunsey might return. Once more he trusts in chance that something will happen to save him. He drinks a lot but still cannot help worrying.

COMMENTARY: The villagers gradually forget about the robbery; the excitement of that event is to be replaced by the excitement of Christmas. But if they forget about the robbery, they do not forget Silas, whom they now regard with pity.

In their attempt to rehabilitate Silas both Mr Macey and Dolly Winthrop urge him to go to church. Silas is not yet ready for this, but he no longer greets his visitors with impatience. George Eliot tells us that he now has 'a sense, though a dull and half-despairing one, that if any help came to him it must come from without; and there was a slight stirring of expectation at the sight of his fellow-men, a faint consciousness of dependence on their goodwill'. The adjectives used (dull, half-despairing, slight, faint) point out that this sense is still very dormant, but it does exist.

NOTES AND GLOSSARY:

skimming-dishes: shallow dishes in which the milk was put so that the cream could be skimmed off easily

pettitoes: pigs' trotters

yarbs: herbs. This is a reference to the cure Silas gave Sally Oates

they took the water just as well: children who have been bewitched by the Wise Woman (see Chapter 2) reacted to baptism in just the same way as other children

the cussing of a Ash Wednesday: this is a reference to a special service (the Commination service) which takes place on Ash Wednesday which is the first day of Lent, the period of fasting in the Christian religion. Sinners are denounced and threatened with God's vengeance

prayer book: the Book of Common Prayer

when leaches were to be applied: in certain diseases, such as blood-pressure, leeches were used to suck the blood from a patient. A doctor used to be called a leech. Squire Cass uses the term metaphorically in Chater 9 when he likens his sons to horse leeches who are draining everything from him

monthly nurse: this was the person who looked after the mother and child for the first month after the birth

I.H.S.: a Greek abbreviation of the name Jesus. It is often taken to be a Latin contraction standing for: (i) *Iesus Hominum Salvator* = Jesus, Saviour of Men; (ii) *In Hoc Signo* = By this sign; (iii) *In Hac Salus* = in this [cross] is salvation. The letters are often embroidered on the priests' vestments or on the altar cloth

the money as comes i' that way . . . like the white frost: there is a combination here of medieval Christian morality and folklore. The church declared it was wicked to work on Sundays, and the money obtained by such work was ill-gotten money. The pagan belief was that such money would turn to dirt or melt like snow or white frost

Athanasian Creed: this creed replaces the Apostles' Creed on major feast days in the church. It is called Athanasian after Athanasius, archbishop of Alexandria in the reign of Constantine

---

Chapter 11

The guests are all arriving at the Red House for the New Year's Eve celebrations. Nancy Lammeter and her sister Priscilla are among them. Everyone admires Nancy, not only for her beauty, but also for her goodness and common sense. After the ladies have dressed in their finest clothes, they go downstairs to the parlour and join the other guests for tea. The Squire is in good spirits and urges everyone to enjoy themselves. He forces Godfrey into asking Nancy for the first dance. Godfrey wants to ask Nancy because he loves her, but is afraid to do so for two reasons: the first is that he is already married and therefore cannot possibly marry Nancy; the second is that Nancy is cold towards him because of his recent behaviour. Although Nancy disapproves of Godfrey, she accepts his invitation rather than create a scene. However, she makes it quite plain to Godfrey that she disapproves of him. Godfrey is undeterred by her coldness and tries to win back her former friendship. He senses that in spite of what she says she is not completely indifferent to him.

COMMENTARY: This chapter presents another picture of life and customs in rural England in the early part of the nineteenth century. In Chapter 6 the picture was provided by the 'low society', in this chapter it is the 'high society' that further helps to fill in the background and comment on the action.

The emphasis is once more on custom, ritual, tradition; the feudal pattern still exists. The dance itself reflects this order, for it consists of a set of fixed patterns and movements which must be obeyed or chaos will follow. So too in society: the Squire must lead the dance; not to do so would be to break the social order, and order is necessary for the stability of the society. There is a deliberate parallel with the religious order and customs mentioned in the previous chapter. This belief in a social hierarchy is held by rich and poor alike. The time when 'Jack's as good as his master' has not yet come.

We meet Nancy Lammeter for the first time and are given some insight into her character. She stands in sharp contrast to the Misses Gunn who think themselves superior but are in fact rather vulgar. The presence of the Misses Gunn is another instance of the gradual, yet increasing, urban influence into the rural areas. By contrasting them with Nancy, George Eliot contrasts urban and rural culture and shows that her sympathies lie with the rural.

NOTES AND GLOSSARY:

joseph: a long cloak worn by women in the eighteenth century, especially when they went riding

the horseblock: a stone block used to help in mounting and dismounting from a horse. They can still be seen today in many places in England, especially outside village churches and inns. In London there is one in Waterloo Place just outside the Athenaeum Club

shortest waists: a dress fashion like that worn by the heroines in novels by Jane Austen (1775–1817). The waistline of the dress was far above where the normal waistline is

skullcap...turban: another ladies' fashion. The skullcap was a light, fitting cap, the front being a piece of false hair attached to the skullcap and worn over the forehead. Over this a turban was worn

sampler: a piece of embroidery worked by young girls in earlier times. It was called this because it was a sample of various stitches the young girl could do. She usually embroidered her name and the date on it and sometimes a pious verse as well

hogsheads: large casks. It indicates wealth and plenty, a state to which Priscilla is used and which she does not want to change

mawkin: a scarecrow

mistletoe bough: it is traditional to hang up a bough of mistletoe at Christmas and the young man may kiss any girl he finds standing under it

old king fell:	refers to the mental illness of George III. He had attacks of insanity on several occasions so it is impossible to say exactly which one this was. One possible date is 1810 when he was replaced by the Prince of Wales as Regent
pigtail:	when the Squire was a youth the young men wore pigtails
breed was stronger than pasture:	the type or breed of sheep mattered more than the food it ate
Sir Roger de Coverley:	a famous folk dance still popular today
charter of Raveloe:	just as it was traditional for the squire to lead the congregation out of church (see Chapter 16) so too was it traditional that he should lead the dance. The hierarchy was sanctioned by hundreds of years of custom and tradition; to break it would be to break the social order
to take tithe in kind:	a tithe is a church tax. The people were allowed to pay this tax in farm produce. In 1836 there was an act which decreed that tithes must now be paid in cash
springe:	active. This is a dialect word from the Midlands and north of England
piert:	another dialect word meaning, cheerful, lively
slack-baked:	half-baked

Chapter 12

At the same time that Godfrey is enjoying his moments with Nancy, his wife is struggling through the snow carrying her child. She is intent on vengeance, because Godfrey has told her that he would rather die than acknowledge her as his wife. She knows that there will be a great party at the Red House; her intention is to go to it, and make the truth about herself and her child known to the Squire.

She is a drug addict and on the way feels a need of the drug. She takes a dose and shortly afterwards the drug has its effect, causing her to relax, and creating in her a desire to do nothing else but to lie down and sleep. This she does in the cold and snow, still clutching her child. The child eventually wakes up, sees a light and toddles towards it. The light comes from Silas Marner's cottage. The door of the cottage is open, there is a bright fire in the hearth and the child falls asleep in front of it. The reason the door is open can be explained by the fact that Silas had taken to the habit of leaving it open on occasions, in the hope that the money which disappeared miraculously whilst the door was not locked might equally well reappear when the door was open. On this particular morning the villagers had told Silas that, because it was New Year's Eve, he must stay up and hear the old year rung out and the new year rung in, because to do so was to bring good luck and, who knows, perhaps he would get his money back. This excites Silas, and causes him to have one of his cataleptic fits; that is the reason he does not notice the child enter his cottage. When he wakes he turns towards his hearth and thinks he sees gold gleaming on the floor in front of the hearth (remember Silas has very bad eyesight). He immediately thinks that his gold has returned and stretches forward to touch it. Instead of feeling hard metal he touches soft, warm curls. He realises that it is a child and at first thinks it is his little sister who had died when she was very young. This makes him think of his early life, and raises thoughts of tenderness in him that had lain dormant for a very long time. He takes care of the child, feeds her and takes off her wet shoes. This makes him realise that she has not entered the house through mysterious means but has walked into it. Picking up the child he goes outside and retraces her footprints in the snow until he comes to her mother, lying on the ground, half covered with snow.

COMMENTARY: This chapter contains one of the coincidences for which George Eliot has been criticised, namely the collapse and death of Molly Farren so close to the open door of Silas Marner's cottage. There is a reason for Dunsey to go to Silas Marner's cottage; there is less reason for Molly Farren to go. On the other hand, there is no reason she should not collapse there. Why Silas has his door open is explained, and so, too, is the reason he does not see Eppie enter his cottage.

We see another instance of the parallels that constantly occur in *Silas Marner*. It was a robbery that led Silas to close his door to mankind; it is another robbery that leads him to open it. The fact that he follows the advice of the villagers shows him to be more susceptible to their influence. It is also significant that it is New Year's Eve. This indicates that a new phase in Silas's life is about to begin.

For a fuller discussion of coincidence and improbable possibility see Part 3.

NOTES AND GLOSSARY:

draughts of forgetfulness: this is a metaphor meaning that Nancy acts upon him like a drug making him forget his worries. Like everything else in the book George Eliot has chosen this metaphor very carefully because at exactly the same time, his wife Molly is literally taking a drug to enable her to forget how miserable she is

Nemesis: the Greek goddess of retaliation—punished, repaying

familiar demon in her bosom: the bottle of laudanum she carried

because that was good luck ... money back again: Q. D. Leavis has a long
        note on 'luck' in the Penguin English Library edition
        of *Silas Marner*. She argues that, in *Silas Marner*,
        luck 'has the status of a pagan superstition or even
        pious belief' and 'is good fortune that always has to
        be deserved' ... 'Luck' she says, 'figures as the inverse
        of Nemesis, the Teutonic fate being appropriate to
        the peasant and the classical to the gentry' (the
        Casses). Godfrey and Dunstan, because of their bad
        deeds, are punished by the Greek goddess of
        retribution, Silas, because of his good deeds, is
        rewarded by the German god of good fortune.
        'There is,' she says, 'an aura of pagan mystery in
        Silas Marner, a belief in the old superstitions.'
        Raveloe is 'a village where many of the old echoes
        lingered'. Silas refuses to replace his old brick hearth
        with a grate and his decision is approved of, for, 'The
        gods of the hearth exist for us still; and let all new faith
        be tolerant of that fetishism, lest it bruise its own
        roots' (Chapter 16)
the invisible wand of catalepsy: catalepsy is likened to a magician who can
        wave a wand and make Silas unconscious

Chapter 13

Godfrey sees Silas Marner carrying Godfrey's own child into the Squire's
parlour; he hears that a woman is dead at the Stone Pits. He is afraid she
may not be dead. He says he doesn't know whose child it is. Silas reacts
strongly against the suggestion that he should leave the child. 'It's come
to me—I've a right to keep it,' he says. Godfrey calls Dolly Winthrop to
aid Mrs Kimble; he waits, wondering if his wife is dead. Then he comes
into the cottage, looks at the dead face, and asks Marner if he will take the
child to the parish. On hearing that he intends to keep the child he gives
him half a guinea and returns home, reappearing in the White Parlour
with a sense of relief. Now he could say tender things to Nancy
Lammeter. Dunsey might betray him if he came back, but Dunsey might
be won to silence. He would see the child was cared for: he would do
everything but own it as his.

COMMENTARY: Godfrey's weakness and selfishness are once more
revealed. His only thought is for his own happiness and comfort. He
lacks the moral courage to own the child as his own. He has shown both a
lack of humanity and a lack of sense of duty and these are the two things
that George Eliot believes every man must have. For one so used to

trusting in chance, he must now feel that this trust has been rewarded. Little does he know that Nemesis is to strike and he is, sixteen years later, to suffer for his neglect of duty and rejection of the gift of the child. On the other hand, Silas accepts the child and is rewarded accordingly. His rehabilitation has now really commenced.

NOTES AND GLOSSARY:

the parish:	the parish administered the Poor Laws. 'To go on the parish' meant that the parish looked after you and send you to the workhouse, a place dreaded by the poor. Eppie refers to this in Chapter 21 when she says the town was worse even than the Workhouse
mazed:	bewildered

Chapter 14

Molly Farren is given a pauper's funeral and no one is there to mourn.

The attitude of the villagers to Silas changes once more, particularly amongst the women. They all offer him advice about bringing up Eppie. The one who helps him most and whose advice he most respects is Dolly Winthrop. Apart from showing Silas how to look after the little girl and giving him clothes for her, she also tells him that he must have her christened and brought up in the religion of Raveloe. Even though this is not the religion of the country where he came from, Silas agrees, for he and the child are now living in Raveloe and they will abide by the customs of the village. He decides that she will be christened Hephzibah after his mother and when Dolly Winthrop says that it is a hard name Silas says it can be shortened to Eppie.

Eppie, like all children, is sometimes naughty, and Dolly advises Silas on certain ways to punish her. Silas cannot, however, bring himself to hurt Eppie, and so she is raised with love and without punishment. She goes everywhere with Silas and the attitude of the village towards him changes completely. Silas is now ready to sit and talk to the villagers and seek their advice on how to bring up the child, and the villagers are equally happy to talk to Silas and give the advice which he seeks.

The presence of the child is slowly transforming Silas's life.

COMMENTARY: This is one of the key chapters in *Silas Marner*. In it George Eliot repeats the message of the Wordsworthian motto she chose for her novel and through the action she fulfils her intention of showing the 'remedial influences of pure, natural human relations'.

NOTES AND GLOSSARY:

robin:	robin red-breast, a small bird which used to seek refuge in homes of the villagers in bad weather

scrat:	scratch for a living
moithered:	worried, bewildered
ringing the pigs:	to put rings in the pigs' noses
'I believe':	the first two words of the Apostles' Creed
'noculation:	inoculation against smallpox
It's a Bible name:	the idea is that if the name is in the Bible it must be acceptable. The meaning of Hephzibah is significant: 'my delight is in her'

he's very sharp, God help him: there was and perhaps still is the belief that there is a touch of the Devil in the clever man

colly:	to blacken, to cover with coal dust
Goliath:	a giant of a man. See the Bible, 1. *Samuel* 17:4–51, where Goliath is slain by the very small and young David
brownie:	a helpful goblin, fairy
lady-birds:	small red and black beetles
city of destruction:	in the Bible this refers to the cities of Sodom and Gomorrah, *Genesis*, 19:15–16. It could also refer to Christian being led from the City of Destruction in the famous allegory *The Pilgrim's Progress* (1678; 2nd and 3rd enlarged editions, 1679) by John Bunyan (1628–88), because at the beginning of the novel Silas with the bundle on his back resembles Christian with his bundle

---

Chapter 15

Godfrey takes a keen but secret interest in Eppie's progress. He gives Silas small gifts from time to time but nothing that would arouse suspicion and he consoles himself with the thought that the child is being well taken care of and it is possible that she is happier being brought up among the poor than among the rich.

Dunsey has not returned and Godfrey feels free from worry. Everyone is happy that he has mended his wicked ways and they all conclude that he will marry Nancy.

For Godfrey, 'the vision of his future life seemed to him as a promised land'. He will marry Nancy and live happily with her and their children.

COMMENTARY: Godfrey, in his weakness and selfishness, can think of no future but one with Nancy and their children playing happily on the hearth at the Red House.

'And that other child—not on the hearth—he would not forget it; he would see that it was well provided for. *That was a father's duty.*'

There is a double irony here. Godfrey in no way assumes a 'father's duty' and sixteen years later when he, in his need, attempts to do so, it is too late.

In rejecting his child Godfrey commits two major sins in the eyes of George Eliot: he has neglected his duty and shown a lack of humanity.

NOTES AND GLOSSARY:

That famous ring that pricked its owner: refers to a French fairy tale, *Le Prince Chéri*. In it there was a ring which pricked the prince's finger whenever he was about to do wrong

Chapter 16

It is now sixteen years since Eppie was found on Silas Marner's hearth. She has grown into a beautiful girl. On her way home from church, she asks Silas if it would be possible for them to have a garden. Silas says that of course she can have a garden, though it will mean some hard work, whereupon Aaron Winthrop, now a young man of twenty-three, who is obviously in love with Eppie, volunteers to make the garden. So it is agreed that Aaron and his mother will come to the weaver's cottage that same Sunday afternoon.

There are many signs of change. Apart from the presence of a dog, cat and kitten, the cottage is filled with good furniture which has been supplied by Godfrey Cass. The villagers find it quite in order that he should help Silas Marner, because he can afford it, and Silas was doing the village a favour by bringing up the child. Silas is now looked upon as an exceptional person who, more than anyone else, deserves the help of his neighbours.

Silas has changed over the years. The fact that he has brought Eppie up in all the ways of the village means that he too is affected, and, more and more, he has adopted the customs of the village, which are very different from the ones he knew when he lived in the Lantern Yard community. Over the years he has told Dolly Winthrop about his past. Dolly is unable to explain to Silas why he should have suffered when he was innocent, but, in her simple way, she gives the same explanation as the wisest believer when she tells Silas that, even though he cannot see the reason, there must have been one, and what he must do is remain good and true to himself and trust in an ever-loving God. Silas agrees and concludes that 'There's good in this world—I've a feeling o' that now'.

Silas has also told Eppie about his past and of his lonely life until she came unexpectedly into it. He has kept her mother's wedding ring and he gives it to Eppie when she grows up. That afternoon they go outside to plan the garden. Eppie goes in search of bricks for the fence and discovers that the stone pit is nearly empty. Godfrey Cass has decided to drain it.

Eppie then tells Silas that Aaron would like to marry her and she is happy about that. Silas is not to worry that they would leave him because Aaron has agreed that they would all live together in Silas's cottage.

COMMENTARY: 'Perfect love has a breath of poetry which can exalt the relations of the least-instructed human beings.'

This chapter stresses the major theme in the book, namely the effect of love, especially the love of a child.

We see the changes that have taken place both in Silas and in his household since the arrival of Eppie sixteen years ago.

NOTES AND GLOSSARY:

lavender: it was traditional for the countryman to plant lavender for his bride. Lavender was used to scent the bed-linen

the weaving was going down too: more and more weaving was done in factories

gods of the hearth: this is a reference to ancient Rome, where the household gods were honoured

mine own famil'ar friend ... heel again' me: reference to the Bible, Psalm 41:9 'Yea, mine own familiar friend, in whom I trusted ... hath lifted up his heel against me'

Chapter 17

Priscilla Lammeter and her father have had lunch with Godfrey and Nancy at the Red House. The Red House is now quite changed; where all was gloomy and neglected before, it is now shiny and well cared for. This change took place fifteen years before, when Godfrey brought Nancy home as his bride and Nancy made her woman's presence felt in the home. Priscilla has never married and takes care not only of her father, but of his farm also. Godfrey has decided to take up dairy-farming (this is why he is draining the stone pits), and Priscilla tells Nancy that this will be good for her, as it will give her something to do apart from attending to the house and garden.

The reason that Nancy needs to be occupied is that she has no children. She had one child but it died at birth, and it is now obvious that she and Godfrey will never have children. She is, of course, upset by this, but not as much as Godfrey. Godfrey has on several occasions suggested adopting a child. The child he has in mind is Eppie, but Nancy has always opposed this because she believes if God wanted them to have children he would have given them children. To adopt a child would be going against God's will and providence. Godfrey dares not tell her that

Eppie is his child; this is a secret he must keep. The fact that he and Nancy have no children seems to him to be a punishment for his earlier wickedness.

On this Sunday Godfrey is out inspecting the reclaimed land and Nancy is at home. There is a disturbance in the village and Nancy wonders what has happened. She has a vague sense of fear and wishes that Godfrey would return.

COMMENTARY: 'The seed brings forth a crop after its kind' (Chapter 9). With sadness and some bitterness Godfrey now realises that he is reaping what he has sown. Sixteen years ago he had renounced Eppie in order to marry Nancy and have children by her. The marriage is a childless one and Godfrey wishes to adopt Eppie. Nancy, for reasons of her own, refuses adoption, and Godfrey is trapped by his own earlier sin of omission, his refusal to acknowledge Eppie as his daughter.

NOTES AND GLOSSARY:

Derbyshire spar: spar is a crystalline mineral. One of the most famous varieties is the 'Blue John', which is found in Derbyshire, a county in England

increasing poor rate ... ruinous times: the Napoleonic War was over, the prices had fallen and many former labourers were out of work

Michaelmas: the feast of St Michael (20 September). One of the Quarter days dividing the year into four parts

Mant's Bible: this version of the Bible was published in 1816. It was given that title because Richard Mant, Bishop of Down, had written the introduction and commentary

transported: to Australia. Britain transported many of her prisoners to Australia during the period 1788 to 1865

raven: a bird of ill omen. It was described by Christopher Marlowe (1564–93), the Elizabethan dramatist, as 'The sad-presaging raven, that tolls the sick man's passport in her hollow beak'

Chapter 18

Godfrey returns home and Nancy can see he is very distressed. He tells her than Dunstan's body has been found in the drained stone pits and that it was he who stole Silas Marner's money. Nancy senses that Godfrey has something else to tell her and waits. Godfrey then confesses that Eppie's mother was his wife and Eppie is his child. He is fearful that

Nancy will leave him and go home to her father. Instead she sadly asks him why he did not tell her this six years before, or, better still, when Eppie was found. Then she could have been brought up as their own child. Godfrey remonstrates that if he had told Nancy then she would not have married him, but Nancy replies that nothing is worth doing wrong for.

Godfrey tells her that he now plans to acknowledge Eppie and bring her up as their child. Nancy warns him that, because Eppie is grown up, things will not be as he wants them to be, but he must do his duty by Eppie and she agrees to go with him to the weaver's cottage that night.

COMMENTARY: In the previous chapter Godfrey revealed a lack of understanding of human character when he thought that Silas would be happy that he, Godfrey, now proposed to look after Eppie.

The same failing is revealed in this chapter. It appears he has underestimated Nancy, for, contrary to what he expected, she would have welcomed the child. This is a bitter moment for Godfrey for he realises he has committed 'an error that was not simply futile, but had defeated its own end'.

Chapter 19

It is evening of the same day and Silas and Eppie are sitting alone in the cottage. Silas's lost gold has been placed on the table and Silas tells Eppie how he used to count it each day and how empty his life had been until she came into it.

'The money was taken away from me in time,' says Silas, 'and kept till it was wanted for you. It's wonderful, our life is wonderful.'

At this moment there is a knock on the door, Eppie opens it, and Godfrey and Nancy enter. Godfrey tells Silas he feels bound to make up for his brother's crime against Silas, and he plans to do this by taking the burden of Eppie off Silas and bringing her up as his own child. Silas is horrified by these words and is too pained and distressed to speak, except to say to Eppie that he will not stand in her way. Eppie turns to Godfrey and Nancy, thanks them, but tells them she could not leave her father, nor own anyone nearer than him. She has no desire to be a lady nor to give up the people with whom she has grown up. Godfrey is frustrated and somewhat irritated; he is used to getting his own way. He had decided that he would not at this stage tell Eppie that he was her father. However, if he is to get his way it now seems necessary to do so, and he does, telling her that he has a claim on her—he is her father. If he thought this would change matters, he is mistaken. Silas is now ready to fight for what he loves, and asks Godfrey why he did not announce this sixteen years ago: 'God gave her to me because you turned your back upon her, and He looks upon her as mine: you've no right to her.'

Godfrey reproves Marner and accuses him of not thinking of what is best for Eppie. Why, if she stays with Silas she might even marry some 'low working man and then Godfrey could never make her well off'.

Eppie has been listening carefully and realises that Godfrey's attitude to the low working man is what his attitude was to her own mother. This makes both Godfrey, and what he offers, repulsive to her. Nancy tries to persuade Eppie that her duty lies towards her real father, to which Eppie replies that she can only think of one person as her father, and that is Silas, of one place as her home, and that is the weaver's cottage, and of one way of life, and that is the life of the simple people of the village. With dignity she rejects Godfrey's offer, declaring that she can think of no happiness without Silas and that no one will ever come between them.

Godfrey and Nancy realise that they have been unsuccessful in their mission and leave.

COMMENTARY: Once more Godfrey reveals his lack of understanding and his insensitivity to the feelings of others. He thinks he has only to go to Eppie, tell her that he is her father and that he will make her a fine lady, and she will come with him. When she refuses, she is reminded of her 'duty' to him. But what of his duty to her sixteen years ago? Once more Godfrey and Silas are compared. It was the act of a 'false' father when Godfrey refused to sacrifice himself for his child. Silas now reveals the love of a 'true' father when he offers to sacrifice his interests for those of Eppie. Eppie sees the truth of the situation and declares that the love she has for this 'old long-loved father' is much stronger and greater than any duty she might have to 'this new unfamiliar father'.

NOTES AND GLOSSARY:

'beauty born of murmuring sound ...' a quotation from one of the *Lucy* poems by William Wordsworth (1770–1850). For further discussion of Wordsworth's influence on George Eliot and *Silas Marner* see Part 3

Chapter 20

Godfrey and Nancy return home and Godfrey acknowledges that Silas was right 'about a man's turning away a blessing from his door: it falls to someone else'.

He decides that he will not reveal that he is Eppie's father, for this will only cause harm. Instead he will do all that he can to help her and 'make her happy in her own way'.

Godfrey is now reconciled to the situation. He finds it just that he should be punished, and there is a feeling that he and Nancy will live in greater peace and contentment.

COMMENTARY: Godfrey shows more understanding of the situation than he has at any previous time. With bitter irony he realises that because he once wanted to pass as childless he must now be childless for ever. He looks upon this as divine retribution and accepts it as such. Events have forced him to realise that 'there's debts we can't pay like money debts'.

NOTES AND GLOSSARY:

it *is* too late to mend: reference to the proverb 'It's never too late to mend', meaning 'It's never too late to change things or yourself'. Godfrey realises that in this case the proverb is wrong

---

Chapter 21

Silas announces to Eppie that he has a desire to visit his old home and the Lantern Yard community once more. He would like to discuss the drawing of the lots with Mr Paston, 'a man with a deal o' light', and thinks that by now perhaps the guilty person has been found.

They set off, on what, for Eppie, is an adventure, but when they get there the town has changed so much over thirty years that Silas wonders if it is the same town. He eventually makes his way to Lantern Yard only to discover that the chapel has disappeared and has been replaced by a factory. No one can give him any information about his old Lantern Yard friends.

Silas returns to Raveloe and tells Dolly Winthrop that he has 'no home but this now'.

COMMENTARY: This chapter shows how impossible it is to return to one's youth. Time does not stand still and change is inevitable, as Silas finds out when he returns to find that Lantern Yard exists no more.

As a social document the chapter illustrates the great changes taking place in England during the thirty years we have known Silas. More and more the country was being industrialised and the great factory towns were growing up. The spinning wheels that once hummed busily in the farmhouses (Chapter 1) are no more. Weaving is going down (Chapter 16). The individual craftsman with a pride in his work is being replaced by machines in the great factory towns. The grimness of these towns and the terrible living conditions are revealed in this chapter. 'Prison Street' is surely symbolic.

One reason for Silas's return was his hope that some light could be thrown on the past events. Dolly Winthrop asks him to bring back 'any

light to be got up the yard as you talk on, we've need of it i' this world'.
Lantern Yard and the religion practised there once provided Silas with
the 'light' by which he led his life. This no longer exists. But Silas has
another light to guide him now: his love of and devotion to Eppie. 'Since
the time the child was sent to me and I've come to love her as myself, I've
had light enough to trusten by'. Here we have an intrusion of George
Eliot's beliefs. Religion as it was practised at Lantern Yard was narrow
and dogmatic and, as we have seen with Silas, was destructive of human
life and happiness. Such religion she would replace with the religion of
love.

Conclusion

It is Eppie's wedding day and everything is as it should be; it is
early summer, the sun is shining, the flowers are blossoming, and Eppie is
beautiful in her wedding dress, provided by Mrs Godfrey Cass, who, with
her sister and father, watches the bridal procession. Godfrey has paid for
the wedding feast at the Rainbow but for special reasons he is not present
to see the wedding. The villagers agree that Silas deserves his good
fortune; he has 'brought a blessing on himself by acting like a father to a
lone motherless child'. And no one disagrees.

COMMENTARY: Again the imagery reflects the situation. Remember the
weather conditions on the night that Dunstan robs Silas. Recall too how
in the previous chapter the darkness, ugliness and gloom of the
industrial city symbolises the misery, unhappiness and evil that exists
there. Here the imagery—sunshine, light, the colours (white, gold)—
symbolises the happiness in store for Silas, Eppie and Aaron.

There are two more instances of dramatic irony. The first is where the
villagers believe that Godfrey helps Silas because it is one of his family
that wronged Silas. This is true, but Godfrey has done Eppie a much
greater wrong. The second instance is when Priscilla looks at Eppie and
remarks 'I could ha' wished Nancy had had the luck to find a child like
that and bring her up'.

Finally the conclusion spells out the message of the book. In true
parable fashion the bad have been punished and the good rewarded.
And through the relationship of Silas and Eppie we have been shown
'the remedial influences of pure natural human relations'.

Part 3

Commentary

The origin of *Silas Marner*

George Eliot has supplied us with a good deal of information about the origin of *Silas Marner* and the intentions she had in writing it. In an entry in her journal for 28 November 1860, she wrote,

> I am now engaged in writing a story . . . which has thrust itself between me and the other book [*Romola*, 1863] I was meditating. It is *Silas Marner. The Weaver of Raveloe.*

Six weeks later she wrote to her publisher:

> I am writing a story which came *across* my other plans by a sudden inspiration . . . It seems to me that nobody will take any interest in it but myself, for it is extremely unlike the popular stories going; but Mr Lewes declares that I am wrong, and says it is as good as anything I have done. It is a story of old-fashioned village life which has unfolded itself from the merest millet-seed of thought.

Blackwood, her publisher, wrote back telling her that from what he had read of the manuscript he found it 'sombre'. George Eliot replied:

> I don't wonder at your finding my story, as far as you have read it, rather sombre: indeed I should not have believed that anyone would have been interested in it but myself (since William Wordsworth is dead) if Mr Lewes had not been strongly arrested by it. But I hope you will not find it at all a sad story, as a whole, since it sets — or is intended to set — in a strong light the remedial influences of pure, natural human relations. . . . It came to me first of all, quite suddenly, as a sort of legendary tale, suggested by my recollection of having once, in early childhood, seen a linen-weaver with a bag on his back, but as my mind dwelt on the subject, I became inclined to a more realistic treatment.

Several days later she sent George Blackwood 'a motto for the title-page'. Given the nature of her story, and her intentions for it, it is not surprising that she chose her motto from Wordsworth's poem 'Michael':

> A child, more than all other gifts
> That earth can offer to declining man,
> Brings hope with it, and forward-looking thoughts.

Wordsworthian and romantic influences in *Silas Marner*

Poetry is the spontaneous overflow of powerful feelings. It takes its origin from emotion recollected in tranquility.

William Wordsworth (1770–1850)

I am certain of nothing but of the holiness of the heart's affections and the truth of the imagination.

John Keats (1795–1821)

The presence of Wordsworth and Romantic beliefs are to be found everywhere in *Silas Marner*. Both George Eliot and Wordsworth believed:

(1)   that the separation of man from his past and nature has a negative effect on him.
(2)   that truth is perceived through the particular. The child perceives this truth. Man may lose sight of it but an innocent child can lead him back.
(3)   in the superiority of the country over the city.
(4)   that simple, lowly people were suitable subjects for literature. When they chose such a character he was then usually a solitary, alienated figure.

Silas is repeatedly described as 'alien', an 'exile'. He leaves Lantern Yard 'with that despair in his soul—that shaken trust in God and man, which is little short of madness to a loving nature' (Chapter 1).

What this departure creates is a loss of awareness of his personal past. 'Minds that have been unhinged from their old faith and love, have perhaps sought this Lethean influence of exile, in which the past becomes dreamy because its symbols have all vanished and the present too is dreamy because it is linked with no memories' (Chapter 2).

Such a state the Romantic writer believes to be completely life-destroying, and so it is for Silas. One incident occurs that might save him and that is when, out of an act of charity, he provides a cure for Sally Oates. This act prompts 'a sense of unity between his past and present life which might have been the beginning of his rescue from the insect-like existence into which his nature had shrunk' (Chapter 2). But this was not to be. In a desperate attempt to have some meaning in life he substitutes gold for human beings, not because of his love of gold but because of his lack of love. His only companions become the faces on the coins. Such an action reduces him first from human to insect and then even further to an inanimate object. He becomes 'withered and yellow', corresponding to the metal he hoards.

The emphasis that the Romantic writers placed on the child was not a sentimental one. It was based on their belief that 'the child is father of the man', that our past is part of our present and both past and present are part of our future. They believed that the affections of the child must be preserved in the man or he will wither and die spiritually. Men who discard these affections and values, Samuel Taylor Coleridge (1772–1834) said, 'exist in fragments. Annihilated as to the Past, they are dead to the Future.'

That this was also George Eliot's belief is fairly obvious from her works. One metaphor that she employs regularly to illustrate the interaction and interdependence of past, present and future and the disastrous results when the childhood memories and affections are neglected is the metaphor of a 'rooted plant'. In *Daniel Deronda* (1876) Gwendolen Harleth's shallowness is attributed to an inadequate seed-bed: 'A human life, I think, should be well rooted in some spot of native land . . . a spot where the definiteness of early memories may be in-wrought with affection. . . . But this blessed persistence in which affection can take root had been wanting in Gwendolen's life.' She points out the positive nature of such roots in *The Mill on the Floss*: 'Our delight in the sunshine on the deep-bladed grass today might be no more than the faint perception of wearied souls if it were not for the sunshine and the grass in the far-off years which still live in us and transform our perception into love.'

Silas's grief over the breaking of his favourite pot showed us that 'even in this stage of withering . . . the sap of affection was not all gone' (Chapter 2). Eppie's arrival is the stimulus that causes the sap to flow freely and bring about the regeneration of the withered trunk (Silas). Through the child Silas is reintegrated into a human community. But it is in keeping with Romantic theory that the regenerative process commences with a reawakening of memories of his childhood. When Silas sees Eppie at first, the past suddenly merges into the present, and he mistakes her for his little sister. Silas feels that 'this child was somehow a message come back to him from that far-off life: it stirred fibres that had never been moved in Raveloe—old quiverings of tenderness'. Since the robbery the people of Raveloe had been considerate and kind to Silas but he had failed to react. It remained for an 'influx of memories' and 'a vision of the old home' (Chapter 12) to stir the fibres of affection that had remained dormant for so long.

Instinctively Silas is aware of the connection between past, present, and future, and he reveals this in his concern for Eppie's upbringing. Once again George Eliot uses the root-tree image: 'Silas began now to think of Raveloe life entirely in relation to Eppie . . . as some man who has a precious plant to which he would give a nourishing home in new soil, thinks of the rain, and the sunshine, and all influences in relation to his nursling, and asks industriously for all knowledge that will help him to satisfy the wants of the searching roots, or to guard leaf and bud from invading harm' (Chapter 14).

She uses it also in connection with Godfrey Cass. He rejects Eppie because he is fearful of being disinherited, for to be so would, he believes, render him 'almost as helpless as un uprooted tree' (Chapter 3). His rejection of Eppie is not only a rejection of his past, it is also a rejection of 'the holiness of the heart's affections'. The irony of the situation is that he actually becomes the very thing he sought to avoid, 'an uprooted tree', his rejection of his past has rendered his present barren, symbolised of course by the fact that he and Nancy are childless.

George Eliot stresses the rehabilitation of the past as a part of the regenerative process. As Silas cared for Eppie and showered his love and affection upon her, 'his mind was growing into memory: as her life unfolded, his soul, long stupefied in a cold narrow prison, was unfolded, too, and trembled gradually into full consciousness' (Chapter 14). Silas's reawakening sensibilities are accompanied by a reawakening memory until he recovers 'a consciousness of unity between his past and present' (Chapter 16).

Chapter 14 is one of the key chapters in *Silas Marner*. In it George Eliot repeats the message of the Wordsworthian motto she chose for her novel and through the action she fulfils her intention of showing the 'remedial influences of pure, natural human relations'.

> God made the country, Man made the town.
>
> William Cowper (1731–1800)

Another very obvious Romantic feature in *Silas Marner* is the preference of George Eliot for the country over the town. Even though there is little mention of the town there is sufficient to give us an idea of what George Eliot's feelings are. First let us look at what characterises both places and then we will be in a position to draw some conclusions.

The country

(1) *The situation:* Raveloe, which is representative of rural England, is untouched by industrialisation, 'the old echoes lingered undrowned by new voices' (Chapter 1). It is situated in one of the most beautiful parts of England surrounded by an unspoilt nature whose beauty is there for all to enjoy. It is far from 'the currents of free industrial energy and Puritan earnestness' (Chapter 3).

(2) *The inhabitants:* The village people are described as hospitable, simple, homely people, a closely knit community where everyone knows everyone else and where everyone helps in time of need or

distress. Consider their kindness to Silas once he appealed to them for help. Remember also one reason for their suspicion of him was that he had rejected their company. 'He [Silas] invited no comer to step across his door-sill, and he never strolled into the village to drink a pint at the Rainbow' (Chapter 1). Such a rejection was an alien act incomprehensible in a community like Raveloe. The Rainbow was the communal heart of the village; to reject it was to reject the whole spirit of life represented by rural England.

(3) *The temple of life:* A slow pace of life, a 'region of carriers' carts and slow wagons' (Chapter 21).

The town

(1) *The grimness of the industrial town:* 'O, what a dark ugly place' said Eppie. 'How it hides the sky!' (Chapter 21). Nature is excluded and destroyed. (Remember that Silas comes from the town.)

(2) *The inhabitants:* Capitalism and industrialisation had bred a spirit of competitiveness and individualism. This is in opposition to the spirit of co-operation which characterised the rural community and is epitomised in Dolly Winthrop. Industrialisation had alienated man not only from the traditional way of life but also from his fellow men. Eppie encounters this when she goes with Silas to his old town only to be greeted with 'noise', 'movement' and 'the multitude of strange indifferent faces' (Chapter 21). The degree of alienation is stressed by the complete inability of Silas to recognise any of the forms of life and communal spirit which he encounters when he comes to Raveloe. The enormous gap between the two ways of life is stressed in Chapters 1 and 2 by the mutual distrust and incomprehension each party has of the other's way of life. What George Eliot is at pains to stress is that the urban industrial worker, like Silas, is deprived of his rightful inheritance, an inheritance that the village people still possess.

(3) *The tempo of life:* 'He isn't in a hurry like the rest' (Chapter 21).

The following chart sums up some of the major differences.

	Country	**Town**
(*i*)	beauty of nature	grimness of industrial town
(*ii*)	community	individual
(*iii*)	mutual help	competitiveness
(*iv*)	absence of middle man	presence of capitalism, the middle man
(*v*)	man controls machine	machine rules man
(*vi*)	sense of order/hierarchy	destruction of both

(*vii*)	religion/part of social order and hierarchy; established church	Puritan evangelicanism; narrow life-destroying dogmas
(*viii*)	pink-faced, brawny men	pallid, undersized men
(*ix*)	celebration of old customs	destruction and suspicion of them

Setting

'It is the habit of my imagination' said George Eliot, 'to strive after as full a vision of the medium in which a character moves as of the character itself'.

The setting of *Silas Marner* presented her with no difficulties. All she had to do was to recreate the world in which she was born, and in which she grew up. Over and above its function of being the world in which her rustic characters live out their lives, the setting has several other significant functions. George Eliot makes skilful use of it, not only to create atmosphere, but also as a symbolic comment on the situation. Like every other element in the novel it has a role to play.

One particular instance of this is the setting of Silas Marner's cottage. It is not an accident that it is placed on the outskirts of the village. This is a deliberate move on the part of George Eliot to show the position of Silas within the community. The position of the cottage symbolises Silas's alienation from the community. Perhaps the best example to illustrate the symbolic role the setting plays is in Chapter 21 when Silas returns with Eppie to the town whence he had come fifteen years before. If the reader is any doubt about the author's preferences for the country, he or she has only to read the opening of Chapter 22. Here we have a sunny morning in rural England and the contrast with the industrial setting of the previous chapter could not be greater.

Structure

Structure is a term used for the organisation of overall design. It comprises all the aspects that go into the making of the work, for instance, character, events, setting, outside and inside forces and influences. The more successful the integration and interaction of these elements, the more successful will be the work of art.

Closely related to structure is plot. Plot is the organisation of events in the work. A unified plot, such as we find in classic Greek drama, is one in which every incident has a role to play and no incident can be left out without destroying the 'structure'. Contrasted with the unified plot is the episodic plot in which the incidents are loosely connected or may even have no connection whatsoever.

George Eliot stands out among her contemporary novelists for her structural craftsmanship. Lord David Cecil comments on this, 'It is very rare for a Victorian novelist before George Eliot to conceive the story as an organic whole of which every incident and character forms a contributory and integral part.'*

The other great novelists of the period, Thackeray and Dickens, and before them, Daniel Defoe (1660–1731), had used an episodic plot. One reason why the other Victorian novelists used an episodic plot was that their novels were published serially, a new instalment appearing each week. This meant that, to keep the readers' attention, they had to end each instalment on a note of suspense. The method of publication imposed a certain pattern on the structure.

George Eliot, however, did not publish in serial form, and therefore her structure was not hampered by its limitations. In *Silas Marner*, as in all her novels, she conceived the story as a whole, carefully shaping her material to create a perfect and unified work of art.

The use of the parallel plots in *Silas Marner* is one instance of George Eliot's craftsmanship. They are skilfully interwoven and apart from showing the contrasting fates of Silas and Godfrey they provide an excellent opportunity of showing how action arises from character. George Eliot is careful to account for the smallest detail, each incident proceeds logically out of the previous one, and each and every one of the structural elements interacts on the other to produce what George Eliot wanted, 'a complete organism'.

Psychological depth and insight

George Eliot is now considered by many to be England's first great psychological novelist. This quality went almost unnoticed in her own day and it remained for the truly great psychological novelists of another generation, the French author Marcel Proust (1871–1922), as well as Virginia Woolf and Henry James, to recognise it.

What is quite clear is that she was unparalleled in her time for the insight she had into the working of her characters' minds. She explores her characters with a depth unknown to her contemporaries. Her characters are not the 'flat' characters that people most Victorian novels. Generally, Dickens's characters can be described as 'flat'. The term a 'flat' character was first used by E. M. Forster (1879–1970), the English novelist. A flat character (who used to be called a 'type') is presented only in outline without much individualising detail, and so can be readily described in a single phrase or sentence. Forster contrasted the 'flat' character with the 'round' character who is a 'complex and fully realised

*Lord David Cecil, *Early Victorian Novelists*, Fontana, London, 1970, p. 16.

individual'. The definitions of 'flat' and 'round' characters are taken from M. H. Abrams.*

There are, of course, some flat characters in *Silas Marner*, for instance, the village rustics, Priscilla Lammeter and Squire Cass, but the major characters, particularly Godfrey and Silas, cannot be described as such in spite of the parallel plots and their relationship to the moral fable. With her major characters George Eliot explores both character and environment and shows how the interaction of these two elements accounts for their fate.

Characterisation

Silas Marner

Silas is introduced as 'a young man of exemplary life and ardent faith'. He is the hero of the book but he is not a hero such as we find in Shakespeare's tragedies. He is a simple, trusting, self-doubting ordinary working man with a deep love of God and his fellow man. George Eliot has chosen such a hero because she wants to make us feel sympathy for ordinary human beings as well as for the great tragic figures. Silas has grown up in the town, where the community life and social order that we find in Raveloe no longer exists. This is one of the reasons that he and many others like him, particularly the poor people, joined the small non-conformist religious communities such as the Lantern Yard group (see section on religion, pp. 53–5). These small religious communities replaced the village community and gave those who belonged to them a sense of belonging. They also restored order to their lives and made them feel secure.

Silas is a weaver who works hard and receives very little money. However, he is contented and happy, because he feels secure. Any extra money he may have he gives to the Lantern Yard community. This gives his life a purpose; he works hard to support not just himself but also his fellow men and his religion.

He has complete faith in God and the community. That is why it is such a terrible blow to him when he is betrayed, first of all by the man he believes to be his best friend and later, seemingly, by God. This changes him from a man 'who had once loved his fellow with a tender love and trusted in an unseen goodness' to one who shuns his fellow men and declares that 'there is no just God that governs righteously' (Chapter 1). The change in Silas's character is not arbitrary; it has been caused by what has happened to him.

He is a bitter man who has lost his faith in God and man. He has also

*M. H. Abrams, *A Glossary of Literary Terms*, Holt Rinehart and Winston, Inc., New York, 3rd edition 1971.

lost his purpose in life. He severs his ties with his past and moves to Raveloe. With no one to love or work for, Silas turns to his money and becomes a miser. Because he works so hard and because he has no joy in his life he slowly withers away and looks much older than he is. This physical withering symbolises his spiritual withering and is George Eliot's way of showing what happens to man when love is withdrawn and a sense of belonging is lost.

Even though Silas becomes a miser and has nothing to do with the villagers, there are several indications that he has not changed completely. His natural sympathy is aroused by the suffering of Sally Oates and he helps her. He refuses, however, to pretend that he has knowledge when he has not; he was and remains an honest man. One other sign that feeling in him is dormant but not dead is when he sorrows over his broken earthenware pot. Having no humans to love he turns his affections to material objects.

These small incidents prepare us for Silas's reaction when his money is stolen. There is no one to turn to but his fellow men. This is the first step along his road to recovery and reintegration once more into a human community. The next step is the entry of Eppie into his life. Through her George Eliot shows the power of the child to restore a lost soul. From being a person whom people feared and mocked he becomes a loved and respected figure. And more important still, Silas regains his faith in God and man.

Silas was and remained an honest, hardworking man. Whatever changes occurred in him were not arbitrary, but were always a result of circumstances. His life shows the potential need in each of us to love and to be loved, and the destructive results when such love is rejected or withheld.

Godfrey Cass

What characterises Godfrey Cass is 'irresolution and moral cowardice' and these are failings that are to remain with him all his life. He is not an evil man but he is a weak one. He will never willingly harm anyone (unlike his brother Dunstan) but he is not strong enough to put another person in front of himself, he will not sacrifice himself for others. For example, he will not declare that he is Eppie's father for he fears that he will lose both his inheritance and Nancy Lammeter. At this stage he tries to convince himself that Eppie might be happier living amongst the villagers than at the Red House. Later when he wishes to claim her as his own, he points out how undesirable it is that she should live with the villagers. But fate has turned against him. What he convinced himself of earlier on has become a reality: Eppie has no desire to leave the village people.

George Eliot does provide some excuses for his behaviour: the early death of his mother, the way he has been spoilt by his father; but she does not consider these things sufficient defence for his actions. In George Eliot's eyes Godfrey commits one of the greatest crimes: he rejects his duty and with this the love of a small child. And for this crime he is punished.

There is no radical change in Godfrey's character; he finally confesses to Nancy, not because he has gained moral strength but rather because he has become convinced that eventually his sins will be found out.

When he rejected Eppie he not only neglected his duty, he also displayed a degree of lack of human sympathy and understanding. He displays this same lack when he goes to Silas and believes that he should be happy to let Eppie leave him. He sees no irony in the fact that he believes that it is Silas's duty to see to it that Eppie lives in the best possible circumstances. What of his own neglect of duty sixteen years earlier?

Whilst there is little change in his character there is some degree of self-realisation. This is brought about by Eppie's and Silas's reactions to his proposal. At last he realises that rights and duties cannot be separated and the fate he suffers now is the result of his own actions many years earlier.

Eppie

Eppie is the least developed of the major characters. We do know that she is a model daughter. Her love of nature and her fondness for animals is one sign of her affectionate nature. The chief object of her affections is Silas and it is she who is responsible for Silas's cure. This is, of course, her main function in the novel: to show the reforming influence of a child.

She shows the depth of her affections and integrity when she refuses to leave Silas. In this scene when Godfrey confronts her with the truth she also shows an intelligent understanding of the whole situation and of Godfrey's rather unsavoury role in it.

One nice individual touch to an otherwise flat character is when she wants to have done something that Aaron hasn't, namely to have visited the town. We are told that 'there was love between the child and the world' and this is something that is easy to believe when we read the story.

Nancy Lammeter

Nancy is presented as a model nineteenth-century housewife who is held in high esteem by the people of Raveloe. Even though she has little education, speaks with a provincial accent and has hands that show she does housework and makes butter, she has the essential attributes of a lady, 'high veracity, delicate honour in her dealings, deference to others and refined personal habits'.

She has a strict moral code (she would have nothing to do with Godfrey unless he reformed) and rigid principles which she will not alter under any circumstances. This can sometimes be a negative virtue, for example she insists that she and Priscilla dress alike even though it makes the latter look ridiculous.

The same rigid adherence to certain ideas, such as her superstitious religious belief that if God had wanted her to have children he would have given them to her, leads her to reject Godfrey's pleas to adopt a child.

She is at her very best when Godfrey reveals that Eppie is his daughter. On this occasion she shows an understanding that transcends her narrow principles. She is not angry with him, nor does she rebuke him. Her only feeling is one of regret. Her sense of duty and obligation would naturally lead her to adopt Eppie, but greater than that is her awareness of Godfrey's need for the child and her love and sympathy for him.

Dolly Winthrop

Dolly Winthrop displays all the virtues of the community spirit. Whenever anyone was in trouble they called upon her—'she's the best woman to get'—and she went willingly to help them.

She is a simple, generous, practical woman, 'a comfortable woman', who has an intuitive understanding of people's needs. This is revealed in her awareness that Silas must look after Eppie himself and she displays a great deal of tact when she offers to help him. She is an uneducated woman who makes no pretence to know all the answers. She does, however, have a deep religious belief in an ever-loving God, in 'Them above' and, apart from Eppie, it is she, more than anyone else, who does most to restore Silas's faith in God and man.

Dunstan Cass

Dunstan Cass is set in direct contrast to Godfrey. Godfrey may be weak, but he is not evil like Dunstan. Even if Godfrey does not place other people before himself his intentions are good and he will not willingly hurt or destroy them. This is not the case with Dunstan. He has all the vices. He drinks too much, gambles, leads a loose life and takes delight in making other people unhappy. There is a spiteful streak in his nature; he obviously resents the fact that he is not the eldest son and this could be one of the reasons for his trying to destroy Godfrey.

Dunstan is a flat character who shows no development. He is the villain one often finds in Victorian novels, and his fate is the one that befalls all such people.

The rustics

These are the villagers who assemble at the Rainbow inn. They perform the same function in the story as the Chorus in a Greek play, that is, they take no action in the story, but they comment on the other characters and the action. In their conversation they supply us with background information about Raveloe and the people who live there. From their conversation we also learn about some of the customs of that period and of the superstitious ideas held by such people.

Silas Marner as a social document

At first glance it is not obvious that *Silas Marner* is a social document but if you look at it more closely you can see that it tells us quite a bit about conditions and customs in England at the time it was set and the changes that take place over thirty years, which is the period of time that the book spans.

When Silas first comes to Raveloe it is a small, isolated, self-contained community where the old feudal order still exists, a part of England yet untouched by 'industrial energy and Puritan earnestness' (Chapter 3). Rich and poor alike take for granted their role in life; they never question their position, each lives and dies 'according to his place' (Chapter 3).

The Squire and his house represent the last vestiges of this feudal society, and the disintegration of his house and family is symbolic of its disintegration. The title dies with the Squire, Godfrey and Nancy are childless, there is no one left to carry on the family traditions which in turn represent the traditions of a whole class.

As in other instances of the breakdown of feudal society the disintegration comes from both outside and inside forces. To a great extent the Squire and people like him are responsible for their own destruction. The chaos in his house symbolises the chaos that exists in the management of his land and the upbringing of his sons. You could also argue that the order that exists in Silas's cottage symbolises the order and efficiency of the new industrial class who are eventually to take over and destroy rural England and people like Squire Cass.

In times of war—in *Silas Marner*, the Napoleonic War—people like the Squire 'could farm badly quite at their ease' and still 'live in a rollicking fashion' (Chapter 1) because prices are always high in wartime. But wars do not last for ever and at the end of the book we hear of falling prices and an increasing poor rate; 'extravagant habits and bad husbandry' have carried 'the race of small squires and yeomen down

[the] road to ruin' (Chapter 3). The Squire and people like him have sown the seeds of their own destruction, they have made no provision for the future, and so fall ready victims to the outside forces that threaten and finally destroy them.

These outside forces have already been mentioned: 'industry and Puritans'. And the coming of Silas to Raveloe, representative as he is of both industry and Puritanism, symbolises the first incursion of these two forces. It is going to take several centuries for social and economic democracy to emerge in England (it still has not done so completely) but in *Silas Marner* we do see the beginnings.

The role of religion in *Silas Marner*

The second half of the eighteenth century saw the rise of the Methodist movement led by the great preacher and religious reformer, John Wesley (1703–91). It was a movement started in protest against what were believed to be abuses in the Church of England.

When the English Church broke from that of Rome it still retained many of the aspects of the latter—notably the retention of a hierarchical system which was paralleled in the social structure. This hierarchical system was something that the reform movement objected to in particular. It believed that authority lay not in the clergyman, the bishop or archbishop, but in personal conviction. The only authority was the Bible. There were soon breakaway movements from the original reform movement and small independent sects such as the Lantern Yard community were established.

The followers of the new religion came mainly from the poor lower classes living in London or the fast growing towns which were created by the Industrial Revolution. They were honest and well-meaning, but were also often ignorant and superstitious and followed the Bible literally. This led to such practices as 'the casting of lots' and the disastrous results such as Silas suffered. It was the narrow religion of Puritanism that almost destroyed Silas.

There were several reasons why this section of society would turn to the new religious movements. First because of their living conditions, which were dreadful (the description of the town in Chapter 21 gives us some idea of this). The poor had two means of escape from these terrible conditions. They could drown their sorrows in drink, and many did—as William Hogarth's (1697–1764) famous picture 'Gin Lane' shows us. Or they could turn to religion in the hope that if they led a good life here on earth they would be rewarded in the next life. One reason for George Eliot's rejection of Puritanism was its stress on reward in Heaven. She believed that it over-emphasised the 'after-life' at the expense of 'the present life' and this she found life-destroying and wrong.

The second reason why the poor, urban workers would turn to the reform movements lies in the need of the individual for a sense of security. Most people are incapable of independent thought. As long as the old traditions and order remained, independent thought was not called for; the pattern of most people's lives was mapped out for them. When the old order of society broke down, as it did in the urban areas, the people had to find something else to supply their needs. They turned to the new religions which became substitutes for the traditional order that had been destroyed. Their acceptance of the new religion was as total and unquestioning as the acceptance of the villagers of Raveloe of the old social order. George Eliot stresses this when she points out in Chapter 1 that Silas's acceptance of religion was a blind, unquestioning one, that 'independent thought' was something 'he had never known'.

The new religions knew they were competing with the old order and traditions. One instance of this in *Silas Marner* is where the Lantern Yard community shows disapproval of his use of herbs as his mother had taught him. They were intent on destroying belief in the old order — one cannot serve two masters.

It is as if the narrowness and soul-destroying nature of the religion parallels the narrowness and both body and spirit destructiveness of industrialised society. The process of disinheritance commenced by the town and industrialised society is further extended by the religion of the 'narrow religious sect' (Chapter 1).

Some historians believe that one reason why England did not experience a revolution similar to the French Revolution was the rise of the religious reform movements. There could, in fact, be two reasons. First the promise of a reward in Heaven might make the people more readily accept conditions resembling Hell on earth. It was because of this that Karl Marx (1818–83), the German founder of modern Communism, called religion 'the opium of the masses'. The second reason is that in the chapel (the name used for their place of worship) there was no hierarchy. Outside the chapel the social hierarchy might exist but inside each man was equal with a right to his own opinion which he was free to express. The trade union movement owes a debt to the non-conformist chapels for it was only one step from religious equality to an attempt at social, economic equality. The newspaper unions in Fleet Street are still called chapels.

The contrast between the two religions is brought out in *Silas Marner*, in particular in Chapter 10 where Dolly and Silas show a complete incomprehension of each other's religion.

George Eliot shows very clearly how the Established Church, the religion of Raveloe, is a part of the social order. The hierarchy in the Church is a reflection of the hierarchy in society. There is no strong individual belief; religion for the people of Raveloe is a social institution rather than a personal relationship between a man and his god as in the non-conformist religions to which Silas belonged at first. One indication perhaps that Silas is restored to his true past, to that of his forefathers, is his return, because of Eppie, to the church at Raveloe.

Silas Marner and the Victorian period

For the reader in the last quarter of the twentieth century *Silas Marner* may appear over-sentimental, too moralistic, and a little contrived (for instance, the appearance of Eppie on Silas's doorstep immediately after his money has been stolen), but the reader must take into account the background and society of the time in which the novel was written. As Lord David Cecil has pointed out, 'To appreciate the art of another period one must, to a certain extent, enter into its spirit, accept its conventions, adopt a willing suspension of disbelief in its values.'*

The Victorians read not only for pleasure but also for moral edification. They demanded that the novel be moral and didactic; the lesson they wished it to teach was that the wicked would be punished and the good (themselves, of course) rewarded. That this was not always the case on this earth troubled them not, it may not have been how things were, but it is how they would have wished them to be. This was to lead at times to contrived plots and sentimental situations but these were readily accepted. Before we condemn the Victorians outright for such attitudes, it would be well to look at our own age. Many of the films and television programmes of today are every bit as contrived, romanticised and non-realistic as the Victorian novels. Each and every age indulges in some form of wish-fulfilment and escapism from the harsh realities of everyday life.

Some of the Victorian novels, like the television programme mentioned above, were written as mere entertainments, providing nothing more than escapism from the dull monotony of day-to-day living. George Eliot was extremely critical of such works of what she called 'silly fiction masquerading as reality'. Such novels could only do damage to real art. Art was not meant to be an escape from life, on the contrary it was meant to provide a meaning and an understanding of life. For George Eliot art had a moral mission:

> If Art does not enlarge men's sympathies, it does nothing morally . . . the only effect I ardently long to produce by my writings, is that those who read them should be better able to *imagine* and to *feel* the pains and the joys of those who differ from themselves in everything but the broad fact of being struggling erring human creatures.†

*Lord David Cecil, *Early Victorian Novelists*, p. 13.

†George Eliot, Letter to Charles Bray, 5 July 1854, in J. Cross, *George Eliot's Life*, Blackwood, London, 1885, p. 279.

She was aware of the criticism of the improbability of certain events in her novels, and in a letter to her publisher refuted this criticism:

> My stories always grow out of my psychological conception of dramatis personae ... I cannot stir a step aside from what I *feel* to be *true* in character. If anything strikes you as untrue to human nature in my delineations, I shall be very glad if you will point it out to me, that I may reconsider the matter. But alas! inconsistencies and weaknesses are not untrue.*

We who are so willing to accept the probable impossibility are less willing to accept the improbable possibility. But George Eliot reminds us, 'inconsistencies and weaknesses are not untrue'.

Parable and moral fable

There is another factor that must be taken into account when we are discussing the question of sentimentality, contrived plots and improbable or probable situations, and that is the special genre to which *Silas Marner* is related. It is called a novel and a novel it is, but it also owes a debt to the parable form. Henry James said that for George Eliot the novel was 'not primarily a picture of life but a moralised fable'. Here you could argue that Henry James is slightly overstating the case. *Silas Marner* is no mere moral 'fairy-tale' but it does have affinities to the moral fable, to the parable form.

Moral fable

It could be useful to look at F. R. Leavis's definition of the moral fable:

> I need say no more by way of defining the moral fable than that in it the intention is peculiarly insistent so that the representative significance of everything in the fable—character, episode and so on—is immediately apparent as we read.†

The relationship of *Silas Marner* to this definition should be obvious. Nothing in the book is superfluous to the message that George Eliot wishes to convey. Every character, situation and event has a role to play in conveying this message. And we, the readers, are at all times aware of this.

Apart from William Wordsworth, the other major literary influence on George Eliot was John Bunyan. There are a number of parallels between Bunyan's *The Pilgrim's Progress* and George Eliot's *Silas Marner*.

---

*George Eliot, Letter to John Blackwood in *The George Eliot Letters*, ed. Gordon S. Haight, Yale University Press, Yale, 1954, Vo.. II, p. 297.
†F. R. Leavis, *The Great Tradition*, Peregrine Books, Harmondsworth, 1962, p. 250.

Both heroes, Christian and Silas, commence their journeys with bundles on their backs, both are fleeing from life-destroying societies, both are lonely, alienated people who must suffer many trials and tribulations before they achieve final happiness. Furthermore, both novels preach the message that the good will be rewarded and the wicked punished. George Eliot does this through a device which is traditionally found in the moral fable. This device is to use parallel plots, in *Silas Marner* that of Silas and Godfrey, to show contrasting fates. By doing this we, the readers, are all the time able to contrast and compare so that the message is brought home very clearly. It is well to remember that though George Eliot may have rejected the narrow dogmas of Puritanism,

> her standards of right and wrong were the Puritan standards. She admired truthfulness and chastity and industry and self-restraint, she disapproved of loose-living and recklessness and deceit and self-indulgence.*

Reading this, and remembering the character of Dunstan Cass, we are not surprised at the fate that befell him.

There is however one significant difference between John Bunyan and George Eliot. In Shakespeare's play *Twelfth Night* Sir Toby asks Malvolio, 'Dost thou think that because thou art virtuous there shall be no more cakes and ale?' Bunyan would have answered 'yes'; George Eliot's answer would be 'no'. Bunyan in true Puritan fashion, like the Lantern Yard community, rejected the cakes and ale. His rejection is reflected in the fact that his hero can only find happiness in a heavenly garden which can only be attained after death.

By contrasting the Lantern Yard community with that of Raveloe George Eliot stresses the right, and indeed, the necessity of man to enjoy this life. Her final affirmation of this is revealed in the fate of Silas. Unlike Christian he has not to wait for an after-life to enjoy his garden. We leave him finally in peace and contentment in

> the world
> Of all of us—the place where in the end
> We find happiness or not at all.
> (Wordsworth, 'The Prelude')

---

* Lord David Cecil, *Early Victorian Novelists*, p. 230.

Part 4

Hints for study

TO BEGIN WITH here are some words of advice which apply not only to *Silas Marner* but to a study of any work of literature.

The first piece of advice is given by Dr Samuel Johnson (1709–84), the great lexicographer, poet and critic. 'The reader,' he says, 'should:

> read on through brightness and obscurity ... Let him preserve his comprehension of the dialogue and his interest in the story, and when the pleasures of novelty have ceased, let him attempt exactness and read the commentators. Particular passages are cleared by notes, but the general effect of the work is weakened. The mind is refrigerated by interruption; the thought is diverted from the principal subject; the reader is weary, he suspects not why; and at last throws away the book which he has so diligently studied.

What Dr Johnson is saying is that the first time you read a book you should try to read it without referring to notes or critical works on it. You may occasionally have to look at your dictionary but you should try to use it as little as possible during the first reading. Usually the meaning of the passage is clear even if there are one or two words you may not know. If you are constantly stopping to look up words and notes, you will not only fail to follow the story properly, but, even worse, you are likely to come to hate the novel. So that from being something that can delight as well as teach, it will become an instrument of torture. And this is not the intention.

The second piece of advice is that you should try first of all to work out your own ideas before you read any criticism. And, if you find you do not agree with what the critic says, you should not immediately change your point of view. Instead you should examine the point more carefully and try to find out why you differ. Having done this, you may then decide to change your own opinion. This does not matter. What does matter is that you have given careful thought to the situation. This approach will lead to a much more thorough performance.

The third piece of general advice concerns the method of studying. Some people will have one method of studying a text, others a quite different one. There is no *one* correct method. The following hints, therefore, although they are made from experience and have all been well tried in practice, represent only one way of studying *Silas Marner*. You yourself may have another.

Suggested study method

The following three stages in studying *Silas Marner* are suggested:

First of all, before starting on the Preliminary reading, look through Part 2, A general summary of *Silas Marner*.

(1) Preliminary reading

The amount of time that you are able to spend on studying *Silas Marner* obviously matters very much. Even if, however, the time is very limited, you are still most strongly advised to start by reading quickly through the whole book. What points should be borne in mind at this stage?

(*a*) Try to get a general idea of the plot, that is, what happens in the book.

(*b*) Find out who the main characters are and get at least a broad idea of their personalities; *without* going into details yet.

(*c*) Who are the minor characters? What part do they play in the plot? For example, what part does Dunstan Cass play in the plot? Why does George Eliot introduce the Misses Gunn in Chapter 11? What is Squire Cass's role in the story?

(*d*) Try to remember—but again not in detail—the main sequence of events.

(*e*) Try to form a very general impression of the relationship between the main characters. What is the relationship between Silas and Eppie? What is the relationship between Silas and Godfrey? What parallels does George Eliot draw between them?

(*f*) What do you think of the minor characters?

(*g*) What do you think is the main theme of the novel? Are there minor themes as well? Does the author have a message, and if she does, what is that message?

(*h*) What is the setting? Does the setting change? Does the setting tell us anything in particular? Does it help to explain the theme of the book?

When you have finished this quick preliminary reading, it is a good idea, after you have closed the book, to think a little now about your general impressions. You could also try to note them down. Having done this, you *should* have:

(*i*) a general outline of the plot

(*ii*) a general idea of the main characters and, possibly, a more vague idea of the minor ones

(*iii*) a general idea of what the author is trying to tell the reader.

You are now ready for the next major stage.

(2) Detailed reading

Before going on to this stage you should:

(a) read through Part 1, The life of George Eliot. This will give you some idea of what the author was like and some clues perhaps to what she believed in and wanted to teach.

(b) read through the *whole* of Part 3, Commentary, to get a general idea of the themes, of the characters in the book, and of its structure.

(c) prepare the outlines of a master-sheet which you will fill in as you read the story for the second time. The master-sheet should be divided up into sections and each section should represent one of the major aspects of the novel. The number of sections you have depends on you. The sections will, or may, vary from one work to another. A suggested master-sheet for *Silas Marner* could be divided as shown opposite.

This master-sheet is not complete. It should, however, give you some idea of how to plan it and what to include. You can choose yourself if you want to write out a section of the relevant quotation as is done in Sections (a), (f) and (g), or simply give the page reference as is done in Sections (b), (c), (d), (e) and (h). You will also find that on occasions the same reference will apply to several sections, that is p. 69, Chapter 2 applies to both (d) and (e). The references are to the Penguin English Library edition of *Silas Marner*.

When you are reading the book for the second time, on each occasion you come across a particularly significant passage which relates to any one of these sections, make a note of it in the appropriate box. The result is that when you have completed the book you have on one page:

(i) an overall picture of the main points,

(ii) these points conveniently collected under separate headings for ready reference.

When material is collected on such a master-sheet it is much easier to see the implications that you might miss if the special points are not singled out and collected. For example, it enables you to pin-point the exact moments when there are changes in Silas's fate, the various points of view of the author and the way they are related, and the changes that take place in society over a period of thirty years.

SUMMARIES: You have now established the general outlines and you have prepared your master-sheet so that you know what points in particular you are looking at. The time has come for a thorough, careful

Master-sheet for *Silas Marner*

(a) Silas

p. 56. His character, exemplary life, ardent faith (Chapter 1)
p. 68. His life had reduced itself (Chapter 2)
p. 92. Yet few men could be more harmless than poor Marner (Chapter 5)
p. 108. This strangely novel situation (Chapter 7)

(b) Godfrey

pp. 76–7. Chapter 3
p. 81. Chapter 3
pp. 118–9. Chapter 8

(c) Minor characters

pp. 95–105. Chapter 6 (The rustics)
p. 134. Chapter 10 (Dolly)
p. 148. Chapter 11 (Priscilla)

(d) Author's point of view

p. 57. Chapter 1
p. 51. Chapter 1
p. 53. Chapter 2
p. 32. Chapter 3
p. 108. Chapter 7
pp 126–7. Chapter 9 (Chance)

(e) Theme

p. 69. Chapter 2

(f) Social document

p. 51. In the days when the spinning wheels hummed busily in the farmhouses (Chapter 1)
p. 53. And Raveloe was a village where many of the old echoes lingered, undrowned by new voices (Chapter 1)
p. 65. Had worked for a wholesale dealer (Chapter 2)
p. 71. It was still that glorious wartime (Chapter 3)
p. 73. Everybody in their household had the best, according to his place (Chapter 3)
p. 121. Fleet, the deer-hound (Chapter 9)

(g) Setting

p. 52. Edge of a deserted stone pit (Chapter 1)
p. 83. Unenclosed ground called the stone pit (Chapter 4)

(h) Irony

p. 38. Chapter 4
p. 91. Chapter 5
p. 117. Chapter 8
p. 177. Chapter 13

and close reading of the text. You should read the book chapter by chapter, and consult the glossary and notes to each chapter in Part 2, Detailed summaries. Moreover, *you* should write out your own summary of each chapter. The process of making your own summary and thus of getting to know the book, thoroughly and completely, is, without any qualification whatever, the essential thing for you to do. Gaining this familiarity is, quite simply, the necessary condition for any further study of the text. Your own summary may differ from the one in the study guide. You may have included more points. This does not matter at all; but your summary should include all the points found in the study guide.

COMMENTARY: You should also make your own commentary. Check the points in your own commentary with the chapter-by-chapter commentary in Part 2. If necessary, supplement your own commentary by including points from these. In addition you should select quotations in order to substantiate your points.

One of the most useful things to learn before taking any examination or writing any essay is not to depart so far from the text that what *you* say has little connection with what the *author* of the book has written. Hence the great importance of being able to choose an appropriate quotation and thus to give the grounds on which you are establishing your argument.

QUESTIONS: You should now have a good idea of what happens in the story and what points matter. You should then write down what questions you think are significant in the chapter and see if you can answer them.

(3) Final revision

Quickly read through the book once more comparing it with those notes, summaries, commentary and quotations which you have by now built up. The aim at this stage is that your attention should be concentrated upon *these*.

Before taking an examination or writing an essay: read through all your notes and your other material. You should by now have become so familiar with the book that you only need to refer to it now and again to check or develop a point in your notes. These have now become the major aid to your study.

During an examination or writing an essay: divide this into four stages.

(*i*) Write down on a piece of paper as fast as possible the ideas that come to you immediately after you have read the question.

(*ii*) Arrange these ideas in a coherent order so that your discussion develops clearly and logically. Plan your opening particularly carefully, likewise your conclusion.

(*iii*) Write your answer out in full.

(*iv*) Read through your answer, check your argument, your language, your punctuation. This final stage is vital and should *on no account* be omitted.

Since time is one of the most essential factors, be continually aware of it. A rough and sensible division of the time you spend on these four stages might work out as follows: (*i*) 20%, (*ii*) 20%, (*iii*) 50%, (*iv*) 10%.

Key quotations

Below is a list of key quotations from *Silas Marner* (Penguin English Library edition). It is not inclusive. You may have others you wish to include because you find them significant. These have been chosen:

(*i*) to help you to recall a particular point and to imprint it on your memory

(*ii*) to prevent you from digressing too far from the text.

You will find that as these are key quotations most of them are likely to occur on your master-sheet. You should be able to identify each quotation, who is speaking, what are the circumstances and what is the significance of the quotation.

(1) Poor Marner went out with that despair in his soul—that shaken trust in God and man, which is little short of madness to a loving nature. (Chapter 1, p. 61)

(2) Yet even in this stage of withering a little incident happened, which showed that the sap of affection was not all gone. (Chapter 2, p. 69)

(3) Our consciousness rarely registers the beginning of a growth within us any more than without us: there have been many circulations of the sap before we detect the smallest sign of the bud. (Chapter 7, p. 108)

(4) Favourable Chance is the god of all men who follow their own devices instead of obeying a law they believe in. (Chapter 9, p. 126)

(5) To any one who had observed him before he lost his gold, it might have seemed that so withered and shrunken a life as his could hardly be susceptible of a bruise, could hardly endure any subtraction but such as would put an end to it altogether. But in reality it had been an eager life, filled with immediate purpose which fenced him in from the wide, cheerless unknown. It had been a clinging life; and though the object round which its fibres had clung was a dead

disrupted thing, it satisfied the need for clinging. But now the fence was broken down—the support was snatched away. (Chapter 10, p. 129)

(6) Silas had inevitably a sense, though a dull and half-despairing one, that if any help came to him it must come from without; and there was a slight stirring of expectation at the sight of his fellow-men, a faint consciousness of dependence on their goodwill. (Chapter 10, p. 135)

(7) The fountains of human love and of faith in a divine love had not yet been unlocked, and his soul was still the shrunken rivulet, with only this difference, that its little groove of sand was blocked up, and it wandered confusedly against dark obstruction. (Chapter 10, p. 140)

(8) the Squire led off with Mrs Crackenthorp, joining hands with the Rector and Mrs Osgood. That was as it should be—that was what everybody had been used to—and the charter of Raveloe seemed to be renewed by the ceremony. (Chapter 11, p. 158)

(9) The thoughts were strange to him now, like old friendships impossible to revive; and yet he had a dreamy feeling that this child was somehow a message come to him from that far-off life: it stirred fibres that had never been moved in Raveloe—old quiverings of tenderness—old impressions of awe at the presentiment of some Power presiding over his life; for his imagination had not yet extricated itself from the sense of mystery in the child's sudden presence, and had formed no conjectures of ordinary natural means by which the event could have been brought about. (Chapter 12, p. 168)

(10) Godfrey felt a great throb: there was one terror in his mind at that moment: it was, that the woman might *not* be dead. That was an evil terror—an ugly inmate to have found a nestling-place in Godfrey's kindly disposition; but no disposition is a security from evil wishes to a man whose happiness hangs on duplicity. (Chapter 13, p. 171)

(11) As for the child, he would see that it was cared for: he would never forsake it; he would do everything but own it. Perhaps it would be just as happy in life without being owned by its father, seeing that nobody could tell how things would turn out, and that—is there any other reason wanted?—well, then, that the father would be much happier without owning the child. (Chapter 13, p. 177)

(12) As the child's mind was growing into knowledge, his mind was growing into memory: as her life unfolded, his soul, long stupefied in a cold narrow prison, was unfolding too, and trembling gradually into full consciousness. (Chapter 14, p. 185)

(13) for the little child had come to link him once more with the whole world. (Chapter 14, p. 190)

(14) God gave her to me because you turned your back upon her, and He looks upon her as mine: you've no right to her! When a man turns a blessing from his door, it falls to them as take it in. (Chapter 19, p. 231)

(15) I wanted to pass for childless once, Nancy—I shall pass for childless now against my wish. (Chapter 20, p. 236)

Revision questions

If you know your text well and read the critical commentary at the end of each chapter in Section 2 and read Section 3, you should find you are able to answer all of these questions:

(1) What is the major theme of *Silas Marner*?
(2) Why did Silas leave the town?
(3) Why was Silas regarded with suspicion when he first came to Raveloe?
(4) At the beginning of the novel Silas says, 'there is no just God that governs the earth righteously, but a God of lies, that bears witness against the innocent' (Chapter 1). At the conclusion of the novel he says, 'There's good i' this world—I've a feeling o' that now' (Chapter 16). What makes him change his mind? What are the events that lead to his regeneration?
(5) There are many instances of the influence of the Romantic writers and Romantic theories in *Silas Marner*. Give two examples.
(6) Discuss George Eliot's use of parallel plots in *Silas Marner*. What is the purpose and effect of the parallel plots?
(7) Give two major examples of dramatic irony in *Silas Marner*.
(8) In what ways may *Silas Marner* be described as a social document?
(9) What are the main differences between the two kinds of religion that are described in *Silas Marner*?
(10) What is the difference between a 'flat' and a 'round' character? Write a brief character sketch on any 'flat' and 'round' character that may be found in *Silas Marner*.
(11) George Eliot was very concerned with the psychological truth of her characters. Give two significant examples of how the action of the person derived from his character.
(12) Write a brief character sketch of any two of the following characters: Dolly Winthrop, Godfrey Cass, Nancy Lammeter.
(13) How does George Eliot use the setting to emphasise her feelings?
(14) George Eliot often intrudes in the novel. What is the purpose of this intrusion and what effect does it have?

Part 5

Suggestions for further reading

The text

Silas Marner, edited by Q. D. Leavis, Penguin Books, Harmondsworth, 1967.

Other works by George Eliot

Scenes of Clerical Life, 1857 (stories)
Adam Bede, 1859 (novel)
'The Lifted Veil,' 1859 (story)
Romola, 1863 (novel)
'Brother Jacob,' 1864 (story)
Felix Holt the Radical, 1866 (novel)
The Spanish Gypsy, 1868 (poem)
Middlemarch, 1871–72 (novel)
The Legend of Jubal and Other Poems, 1874
Daniel Deronda, 1876 (novel)
Impressions of Theophrastus Such, 1879 (essays)

Biography and criticism

BENNETT, JOAN: *George Eliot: Her Mind and Her Art*, Cambridge University Press, Cambridge, 1949. The first section of this book is concerned with George Eliot's life and its relevance to her work. It is a valuable introduction to the second section which examines her art as a novelist.

CECIL, LORD DAVID: *Early Victorian Novelists*, Constable, London, 1934; Fontana, London, 1970. This deals not only with George Eliot but also with the other Victorian novelists and discusses George Eliot's place in the development of the novel.

COOPER, LETTICE: *George Eliot*, Longman, London, 1951. A very brief but informative introduction to George Eliot's life and works.

HAIGHT, GORDON S. (ED.): *A Century of George Eliot Criticism*, Methuen, London, 1966. A selection of criticism on George Eliot covering a period of one hundred years.

HAIGHT, GORDON S. (ED.): *The George Eliot Letters*, 9 vols, Yale University Press, Yale, 1952–6. This is the most valuable source of information about George Eliot's life and her ideas.

HARDY, BARBARA: *The Novels of George Eliot*, Athlone Press, London, 1959. Contains individual chapters on each of the novels using the 'new criticism' method.

LASKI, MARGHANITA: *George Eliot and Her World*, Thames and Hudson, London, 1973. Contains 123 illustrations and these, together with the text, make an excellent book on the subject.

LEAVIS, F. R.: *The Great Tradition*, Chatto and Windus, London, 1948. One of the most influential books written on the English novel. It contains a study of George Eliot, Henry James, and Joseph Conrad.

WILLEY, BASIL: *Nineteenth Century Studies: Coleridge to Matthew Arnold*, Chatto and Windus, London, 1955. An excellent study of the ideas of the nineteenth century and George Eliot's place in them.

The author of these notes

ANNA RUTHERFORD is a graduate of the University of Newcastle, New South Wales. She has taught in Australia, England and America, and, since 1966, in Denmark, where she is in charge of Commonwealth Studies at Aarhus University. She is Chairman of the European Branch of the Association for Commonwealth Literature and Language Studies, editor of *Kunapipi* and director of Dangaroo Press.

Her published works include *Common Wealth*; she is co-editor, with Donald Hannah, of *Commonwealth Short Stories*, and, with Kirsten Holst Petersen, of *Enigma of Values*, a work of criticism on the Guyanese writer Wilson Harris.

York Notes: list of titles

CHINUA ACHEBE
Things Fall Apart
EDWARD ALBEE
Who's Afraid of Virginia Woolf?
ANONYMOUS
Beowulf
Everyman
W H AUDEN
Selected Poems
JANE AUSTEN
Emma
Mansfield Park
Northanger Abbey
Persuasion
Pride and Prejudice
Sense and Sensibility
SAMUEL BECKETT
Waiting for Godot
ARNOLD BENNETT
The Card
JOHN BETJEMAN
Selected Poems
WILLIAM BLAKE
Songs of Innocence, Songs of Experience
ROBERT BOLT
A Man For All Seasons
HAROLD BRIGHOUSE
Hobson's Choice
ANNE BRONTË
The Tenant of Wildfell Hall
CHARLOTTE BRONTË
Jane Eyre
EMILY BRONTË
Wuthering Heights
ROBERT BROWNING
Men and Women
JOHN BUCHAN
The Thirty-Nine Steps
JOHN BUNYAN
The Pilgrim's Progress
BYRON
Selected Poems
GEOFFREY CHAUCER
Prologue to the Canterbury Tales
The Clerk's Tale
The Franklin's Tale
The Knight's Tale
The Merchant's Tale
The Miller's Tale
The Nun's Priest's Tale

The Pardoner's Tale
The Wife of Bath's Tale
Troilus and Criseyde
SAMUEL TAYLOR COLERIDGE
Selected Poems
SIR ARTHUR CONAN DOYLE
The Hound of the Baskervilles
WILLIAM CONGREVE
The Way of the World
JOSEPH CONRAD
Heart of Darkness
STEPHEN CRANE
The Red Badge of Courage
BRUCE DAWE
Selected Poems
DANIEL DEFOE
Moll Flanders
Robinson Crusoe
WALTER DE LA MARE
Selected Poems
SHELAGH DELANEY
A Taste of Honey
CHARLES DICKENS
A Tale of Two Cities
Bleak House
David Copperfield
Great Expectations
Hard Times
Oliver Twist
The Pickwick Papers
EMILY DICKINSON
Selected Poems
JOHN DONNE
Selected Poems
GERALD DURRELL
My Family and Other Animals
GEORGE ELIOT
Middlemarch
Silas Marner
The Mill on the Floss
T. S. ELIOT
Four Quartets
Murder in the Cathedral
Selected Poems
The Cocktail Party
The Waste Land
J. G. FARRELL
The Siege of Krishnapur
WILLIAM FAULKNER
The Sound and the Fury

HENRY FIELDING
Joseph Andrews
Tom Jones

F. SCOTT FITZGERALD
Tender is the Night
The Great Gatsby

GUSTAVE FLAUBERT
Madame Bovary

E. M. FORSTER
A Passage to India
Howards End

JOHN FOWLES
The French Lieutenant's Woman

JOHN GALSWORTHY
Strife

MRS GASKELL
North and South

WILLIAM GOLDING
Lord of the Flies
The Spire

OLIVER GOLDSMITH
She Stoops to Conquer
The Vicar of Wakefield

ROBERT GRAVES
Goodbye to All That

GRAHAM GREENE
Brighton Rock
The Heart of the Matter
The Power and the Glory

WILLIS HALL
The Long and the Short and the Tall

THOMAS HARDY
Far from the Madding Crowd
Jude the Obscure
Selected Poems
Tess of the D'Urbervilles
The Mayor of Casterbridge
The Return of the Native
The Woodlanders

L. P. HARTLEY
The Go-Between

NATHANIEL HAWTHORNE
The Scarlet Letter

SEAMUS HEANEY
Selected Poems

ERNEST HEMINGWAY
A Farewell to Arms
The Old Man and the Sea

SUSAN HILL
I'm the King of the Castle

BARRY HINES
Kes

HOMER
The Iliad
The Odyssey

GERARD MANLEY HOPKINS
Selected Poems

TED HUGHES
Selected Poems

ALDOUS HUXLEY
Brave New World

HENRIK IBSEN
A Doll's House

HENRY JAMES
The Portrait of a Lady
Washington Square

BEN JONSON
The Alchemist
Volpone

JAMES JOYCE
A Portrait of the Artist as a Young Man
Dubliners

JOHN KEATS
Selected Poems

PHILIP LARKIN
Selected Poems

D. H. LAWRENCE
Selected Short Stories
Sons and Lovers
The Rainbow
Women in Love

HARPER LEE
To Kill a Mocking-Bird

LAURIE LEE
Cider with Rosie

CHRISTOPHER MARLOWE
Doctor Faustus

HERMAN MELVILLE
Moby Dick

THOMAS MIDDLETON *and*
   WILLIAM ROWLEY
The Changeling

ARTHUR MILLER
A View from the Bridge
Death of a Salesman
The Crucible

JOHN MILTON
Paradise Lost I & II
Paradise Lost IV & IX
Selected Poems

V. S. NAIPAUL
A House for Mr Biswas

ROBERT O'BRIEN
Z for Zachariah

SEAN O'CASEY
Juno and the Paycock

GEORGE ORWELL
Animal Farm
Nineteen Eighty-four

JOHN OSBORNE
  Look Back in Anger
WILFRED OWEN
  Selected Poems
ALAN PATON
  Cry, The Beloved Country
THOMAS LOVE PEACOCK
  Nightmare Abbey and *Crotchet Castle*
HAROLD PINTER
  The Caretaker
SYLVIA PLATH
  Selected Works
PLATO
  The Republic
ALEXANDER POPE
  Selected Poems
J. B. PRIESTLEY
  An Inspector Calls
WILLIAM SHAKESPEARE
  A Midsummer Night's Dream
  Antony and Cleopatra
  As You Like It
  Coriolanus
  Hamlet
  Henry IV Part I
  Henry IV Part II
  Henry V
  Julius Caesar
  King Lear
  Macbeth
  Measure for Measure
  Much Ado About Nothing
  Othello
  Richard II
  Richard III
  Romeo and Juliet
  Sonnets
  The Merchant of Venice
  The Taming of the Shrew
  The Tempest
  The Winter's Tale
  Troilus and Cressida
  Twelfth Night
GEORGE BERNARD SHAW
  Arms and the Man
  Candida
  Pygmalion
  Saint Joan
  The Devil's Disciple
MARY SHELLEY
  Frankenstein
PERCY BYSSHE SHELLEY
  Selected Poems
RICHARD BRINSLEY SHERIDAN
  The Rivals

R. C. SHERRIFF
  Journey's End
JOHN STEINBECK
  Of Mice and Men
  The Grapes of Wrath
  The Pearl
LAURENCE STERNE
  A Sentimental Journey
  Tristram Shandy
TOM STOPPARD
  Professional Foul
  Rosencrantz and Guildenstern are Dead
JONATHAN SWIFT
  Gulliver's Travels
JOHN MILLINGTON SYNGE
  The Playboy of the Western World
TENNYSON
  Selected Poems
W. M. THACKERAY
  Vanity Fair
J. R. R. TOLKIEN
  The Hobbit
MARK TWAIN
  Huckleberry Finn
  Tom Sawyer
VIRGIL
  The Aeneid
ALICE WALKER
  The Color Purple
KEITH WATERHOUSE
  Billy Liar
EVELYN WAUGH
  Decline and Fall
JOHN WEBSTER
  The Duchess of Malfi
OSCAR WILDE
  The Importance of Being Earnest
THORNTON WILDER
  Our Town
TENNESSEE WILLIAMS
  The Glass Menagerie
VIRGINIA WOOLF
  Mrs Dalloway
  To the Lighthouse
WILLIAM WORDSWORTH
  Selected Poems
WILLIAM WYCHERLEY
  The Country Wife
W. B. YEATS
  Selected Poems

York Handbooks: list of titles

YORK HANDBOOKS form a companion series to York Notes and are designed to meet the wider needs of students of English and related fields. Each volume is a compact study of a given subject area, written by an authority with experience in communicating the essential ideas to students at all levels.

AN INTRODUCTORY GUIDE TO ENGLISH LITERATURE
by MARTIN STEPHEN

PREPARING FOR EXAMINATIONS IN ENGLISH LITERATURE
by NEIL MCEWAN

READING THE SCREEN
An Introduction to Film Studies
by JOHN IZOD

ENGLISH POETRY
by CLIVE T. PROBYN

ENGLISH USAGE
by COLIN G. HEY

ENGLISH GRAMMAR
by LORETO TODD

AN INTRODUCTION TO LINGUISTICS
by LORETO TODD

AN INTRODUCTION TO LITERARY CRITICISM
by RICHARD DUTTON

A DICTIONARY OF LITERARY TERMS
by MARTIN GRAY

STUDYING CHAUCER
by ELISABETH BREWER

STUDYING SHAKESPEARE
by MARTIN STEPHEN *and* PHILIP FRANKS

STUDYING JANE AUSTEN
by IAN MILLIGAN

STUDYING THE BRONTËS
by SHEILA SULLIVAN

STUDYING CHARLES DICKENS
by K. J. FIELDING

STUDYING THOMAS HARDY
by LANCE ST JOHN BUTLER

A CHRONOLOGY OF ENGLISH LITERATURE
by MARTIN GRAY

A DICTIONARY OF BRITISH AND IRISH AUTHORS
by ANTONY KAMM

AN A.B.C. OF SHAKESPEARE
by P. C. BAYLEY

THE METAPHYSICAL POETS
by TREVOR JAMES

THE AGE OF ROMANTIC LITERATURE
by HARRY BLAMIRES